How to Self-Learn:
Teach Yourself Anything, Become an Expert, and Memorize Everything

By Peter Hollins, Author and Researcher at petehollins.com

Table of Contents

CHAPTER 1: NECESSARY ATTITUDES FOR RAPID SELF-LEARNING — 7

- LEARNING MISCONCEPTIONS — 7
- LEARNING MINDSETS — 16
- REFLECTIVE LEARNING THROUGH THE GIBBS MODEL — 25
- UNDERSTAND COGNITIVE LOAD AND WORKING MEMORY — 33
- GAMIFICATION — 41
- INTRINSIC MOTIVATION — 48

CHAPTER 2: JUST THE BASICS? READING, NOTE-TAKING, AND WRITING — 55

- SQ3R METHOD — 55
- 3-2-1 STRATEGY — 62
- FRAYER MODEL — 68
- SEMANTIC FEATURE ANALYSIS — 75
- NOVEL NOTETAKING STRATEGIES — 82
- R.A.F.T. — 89

CHAPTER 3: REMEMBER ANYTHING — 99

- RETRIEVAL PRACTICE — 99
- INTERLEAVING — 106
- CHUNKING — 113
- LEARN BY MAKING ASSOCIATIONS — 119

CHAPTER 4: HOW TO DEEPLY EMBED NEW KNOWLEDGE — 129

- THE FEYNMAN TECHNIQUE — 129
- ANALOGIES — 135
- USE GRAPHIC ORGANIZERS — 140
- CONNECT, EXTEND, CHALLENGE — 148

CHAPTER 5: THE BIGGER PICTURE OF USING YOUR KNOWLEDGE — 157

- KWL — 157
- TRIANGLE-SQUARE-CIRCLE — 162
- BUILD A SECOND BRAIN — 169

SUMMARY GUIDE — 185

Chapter 1: Necessary Attitudes for Rapid Self-Learning

LEARNING MISCONCEPTIONS

Whether you are studying for an important exam or simply working toward your self-development goals, knowing *how* to learn will be an important determiner of your success. Perhaps one of the biggest problems with effective learning is not that people lack the memory, skills, or intelligence to learn—it's that they lack the knowledge of how to do it properly. Even experienced teachers and professionals can have outdated and unfounded assumptions about the best way to encourage the human brain to learn as much as it can.

In this book, we'll be looking at ways to shift your attitude toward the learning process so that you can not only be more effective at reading, taking notes, remembering, and staying organized, but also be more capable of deeper conceptual understanding. We will consider not only handy tips and tricks, but also take a closer look at the attitudes, mindsets, and overall principles that underpin genuine learning.

First, though, we'll consider what stands in the way of effective learning: the popular misconceptions about what learning is and how it happens.

The evidence-based scientific facts tell us that our conventional understanding about learning is sometimes wrong. For example, a study by Simons and Chabris in 2011 found that people believed that the memory "works like a video camera," whereas there is zero empirical evidence to support this idea. Here are some other common myths to drop before we continue to more evidence-based strategies and approaches in the remaining chapters:

Myth 1: To learn better, study for a longer time.

Wrong! The phrase "work smarter not harder" comes to mind. Are you one of those people who looks up at the clock at the end of a grueling study session and considers it a success if a lot of time has passed? Do you write "study two hours" on your to-do list? This myth is a lot more pervasive than it first appears, but it may hint at a misunderstanding of how the brain actually works. It sounds obvious, but merely putting in the hours at your desk is not the same as truly grasping material, storing it, and remembering it for the long term.

Myth 2: Students know best.

In fact, you may be a poor judge of how well you're learning, and not great at self-regulating your study. Without knowing it, you may avoid challenging material. Hartwig and Dunlosky (2012) found that students often choose strategies with zero scientific backing, and Kornell and Bjork (2007) claim that students' "intuition" about the best approach is not usually trustworthy.

Maybe you're going through some vocabulary flip cards or practicing math problems. You may decide that you've practiced enough, but could that just be your laziness talking?

Myth 3: If you've learned it, you'll remember it.

When it comes to memory, many of us assume that once something is drilled into memory, it stays there. But cognitive researchers and learning scientists have discovered that the memory is a complicated, dynamic process. Your natural tendency is actually to forget, unless you're actively trying to avoid it. Some estimates have us forgetting around eighty percent of what we've learned within one or two weeks. Unless we deliberately do something to mitigate the effects of this "forgetting curve" we will never properly retain information, and we can never be said to have properly learned anything. However, if we don't understand how memory actually works in the first place, we may be vainly studying away, unaware of the fact that we are committing barely any of it to memory.

Myth 4: To learn something, drill it over and over again.

Similarly, your ability to recall information in the short term is a poor predictor of how well you'll remember it in the longer term (Soderstrom & Bjork, 2015), so you can't assume you've learned something just because you repeated it plenty of times during a study hour. You've probably had this experience before: you rehearse a piece of information over and over and really do feel like you've "got it." Yet when you take your exam the next day, your mind is blank. Why? We'll explore the answer in later chapters, as well as consider the value of "interleaved" practice, spacing, and repetition.

Myth 5: Reading is more useful than practice tests.

Roediger and Karpicke (2006) found that it's the other way around: practice testing is more effective than re-reading material. This is because when you test yourself, you're practicing retrieval, whereas re-reading does not allow you to glean anything new.

Myth 6: It's important to set up the perfect study space.

Partly true, but learning researcher Robert Bjork believes that we form stronger associations (and therefore better memories) when we learn in diverse locations, rather than the same spot each time.

Myth 7: Practice, practice, practice.

Effective memories are not formed from repetition alone. In the 1960s, educators believed that rehearsal and repetition were enough, but today it's understood that memory is more complicated than that. While repetition helps a little, more meaningful data is more easily recalled, meaning that *how* we repeat and rehearse information matters as much as *how often* we repeat it.

Myth 8: Each of us has our own "learning style."

You've probably heard of the idea that some people are more verbal learners, for example, or that others do better with information presented aurally or visually. Despite its popularity in the common imagination, learning styles may be a myth; the American Psychological Association published a report in 2019 stating that belief in individual learning styles may actually get in the way of students' learning, rather than improve it. If you're thinking about using only those strategies that fit best with your presumed style of learning, don't worry: the techniques with the most scientific backing can be used effectively by everyone.

Myth 9: "The left brain does this; the right brain does that..."

In a similar vein, there is little evidence to suggest any difference between "left-brained" activities or individuals and "right-brained." The left is purportedly oriented toward math and language, while the right brain is more about creativity. The truth is this is a complete myth.

Perhaps the biggest and most damaging myth, however, is the following:

Myth 10: Students will automatically and intuitively pick the right way to study.

This book is about learning to learn, which is not something that schools teach. Do not assume that you already know what the best way to learn is. When you think about it, you may have some fixed ideas about the natural way to progress with your studying. But where did you pick up these ideas? Do you really have any evidence that they work?

Most likely, your current approach is one of habit that you never really questioned. However, not all studying is created equal, and you *cannot* trust yourself to learn well by accident! Instead, it makes sense to closely consider the evidence-backed techniques out there, and train ourselves to use them rather than default to ingrained habits that may not be helping us.

You picked up this book for a reason. In all likelihood, on some level you are trying to improve the way you currently learn because you know you could be better—but you're not sure how yet. One good step to begin with is to ask:

Q: How have you studied and learned new things in the past? For example, did you sit down, plonk a book on your lap, and re-read your textbook with a highlighter in one hand? Did you start automatically making notes, or did you begin by first drawing up a study timetable of how many hours you would need to devote?

Q: Now ask, how well has this worked for you? Be honest and appraise how well the above technique has actually been serving you. Do you largely feel like you retain what you learn, that you have a good grasp of new material and that you are using your time and energy well?

If most of us are honest, we have never even asked ourselves these two questions in the first place! But it can be illuminating to realize that your current approach may not be working as well as you think it is. This is where this book can help. Too much study advice out there never challenges the learning myths we buy into as a culture, and in fact may only reinforce them.

As you read the chapters that follow, try to keep an open mind and try to imagine that your new learning approach could be quite different from your old one. If you find yourself reverting to old methods, remind yourself of the above questions and your answers. It may be comfortable and easy to default to tired old habits, but in the end, this will not help you fulfil your full potential, be as effective as you can, and use the time you have most wisely.

LEARNING MINDSETS

Okay, so we've thrown our myths and misconceptions about learning out the window. We're going to forget the old learning approaches we've been taught in school and embrace a smarter approach. Time to dive into some clever techniques, right? While this seems like a good idea, it's far better to understand that **self-directed learning is as much about useful methods as it is about attitude, mood, perception, and feeling.**

For example, you could have the most scientifically sound approach, but if you are unmotivated, it doesn't matter. Let's take a look at Six Sigma strategy author Tanmay Vora's famous "3 Ls of self-directed learning," which couldn't be more different from the approach taught in schools. (There is in fact one school launched in the 90s, the Brisbane Independent School, that bases its curriculum around these principles, but if you weren't lucky enough to go there, you can always learn their approach below!)

Seven characteristics are emphasized in this model:

- Playfulness
- Autonomy
- Internalized Evaluation
- Openness to Experience
- Intrinsic Motivation
- Self-Acceptance
- Flexibility

The idea is to develop your own ability to self-direct and self-regulate. In other words, to become your own teacher. A self-directed learner is not just someone who is aping a series of useful techniques; rather, they have learned how to learn, and they do it well. They take initiative, adapt, persevere, and remain curious. Basically, they foster an *attitude of learning* that goes beyond any particular subject or activity.

The exact study techniques you use matter, but what's most important is your mindset. With the correct attitude, you pace yourself, spring back from disappointment or difficulty, adjust as you go, set your own goals, and feel empowered when you reach them. Your motivation and sense of purpose is stronger because you guide yourself.

Compare the following students:

Student A: Wants the teacher to tell them what to learn and how. Then they hack away at it, at home alone, wasting time on techniques that don't get them very far. They don't care about anything outside the curriculum. When they do poorly on a test, they blame the teacher for not being better.

Student B: Takes the initiative to make their own study curriculum and works in collaboration with others to continuously refine it so that they're using their time in the best way possible. They keep learning even after an exam and beyond the curriculum, and when something doesn't work, they take responsibility for it, determining a better way forward instead.

Student B is a self-directed learner, while student A is arguably not learning anything.

Student B can reflect on their process, can use their time efficiently, and is motivated from a sense of personal responsibility and inquisitiveness.

How do you develop such a mindset?

Identify Your Goals

You need realistic yet challenging goals that let you know what you're trying to achieve in the first place. These are not just immediate goals regarding the content itself ("I want to understand chapter 5") but broader goals about your development as a student of life ("I want to be more resilient when receiving critical feedback from others").

Stay Curious

Keep asking questions, and don't take everything at face value. Why did XYZ happen? What would have happened if you did something different? A lifelong, self-directed learner places curiosity at the center of everything they do.

Challenge Yourself

Growth and learning take place outside your comfort zone. Push yourself to do more—the sense of reward and accomplishment will be greater, and this feeling of meaning will motivate you to carry on. If the goals that others assign to you are on the conservative side, set your own, more ambitious goals. That said, a goal that is too ambitious will overwhelm you and leave you feeling discouraged. It's your job, however, to find the perfect spot in between!

Track Your Progress

You need a way to measure your effectiveness and monitor your progress. Set a standard and regularly ask how you measure up against standard. Again, you don't need to wait for others to test or appraise you; you can do it yourself. For example, set yourself a weekly quiz and keep track of your scores.

Pay Attention to Your Source of Motivation

Students may budget their time, and they may juggle their energy levels, but remember also to be mindful of your degree of motivation and, more importantly, where that motivation is coming from. Ideally, you want to be *intrinsically motivated*, i.e., have a drive to do something that comes from your own inner determination and personal values rather than external rewards. Your goals need to genuinely mean something to you or your motivation will fizzle out. Some self-directed students choose to have their mission statement or overall goal hung on a poster above their desk so they're constantly reminded of their "big why."

Value Progress, Not Perfection

We cannot guarantee any particular outcome, but we can always choose our actions in the moment. By focusing on what is in our control as we progress through the learning process, we stay empowered. Furthermore, avoid comparing yourself against others, and simply keep asking yourself: am I better than I was before?

Reach Out to Others

There are limits to sitting alone and learning. Reach out to others and collaborate, learn together, ask questions, seek feedback, be challenged and inspired, and compare your process. Find those who share your goals and support one another to reach them. This is an aspect of motivation that modern school systems undervalue.

Hopefully you're beginning to see the difference between a superficial and ineffective learner, and a more engaged, more self-directed genuine learner. Maybe you think, "I don't need to be a deep learner; I just want to pass my exam." Well, the secret is that whatever your learning goals, you will achieve more if you adopt the mindset of those people who have a lifelong love of learning.

One excellent way of taking responsibility for your learning journey is to keep a diary. This "learning journal" can be used to keep tabs on yourself, track your progress, record feelings and developments, ask questions, and strategize. There are two important things to remember:

- Make your journal relevant to YOU and your learning goals
- Check in with it regularly—for example, at the end of every day or week

As your first entry in the learning journal, write down your primary goal. Make sure the goal is challenging but still realistic. Also make sure you know how you will track the goal—how will you be sure you have achieved it?

Your goal may need to be broken down into smaller sub goals. For example, your main aim may be to "learn Spanish," but this consists of several subgoals of passing a particular test, having a conversation with a native in Spain, or being able to read a certain text with a certain level of fluency. Remember, though, that these goals are only part of the story. Also include goals that refer to the learning process itself; for example, you may wish to improve your short-term memory, be more organized with your study materials, and build better confidence.

The more time you take fleshing out your goals in your journal, the better you'll be able to monitor those goals when you return to your journal periodically, whether that's once a day, once a week, or even once a month.

Let's say that at the end of each day you check in with your learning journal. You remind yourself of your main goal and reconnect to your reason for wanting to achieve it. You look at what you've done that day and appraise your progress. What have you achieved? What would be done better tomorrow? Maybe you tackle an attitude or mindset problem or maybe you simply tweak a practical matter by trying a different tactic going forward.

Whatever you choose to do with your journal, just remember to make sure it works for YOU and your learning goals and that you are routinely checking in with it to realign with your goals and monitor your progress. Don't be too hard on yourself when you start out. Remember the seven characteristics of a self-directed learner:

- Playfulness – make it fun! Stay curious.
- Autonomy – take responsibility; don't wait for others to give you permission or direction.
- Internalized Evaluation – set your own standards, then follow them.
- Openness to Experience – be open to new ways of doing things.
- Intrinsic Motivation – regularly ask yourself **why** you are aiming for your goals.
- Self-Acceptance – forgive small missteps and be patient as you figure things out.

- Flexibility – if something doesn't work, it's not a problem; just keep asking questions until you find something that does.

With practice, your learning journal can be a powerful tool that helps you take charge of your learning and develop an optimal mindset. As you encounter techniques in the following pages, you can appraise them, test them, and evaluate them for yourself in your journal. If you can do this consistently, congratulations—you are now learning like a self-directed learner does!

REFLECTIVE LEARNING THROUGH THE GIBBS MODEL

The best students *in* the classroom are those who are the best students *outside* the classroom.

"It is not sufficient simply to have an experience in order to learn. Without **reflecting** upon this experience, it may quickly be forgotten or its learning potential lost. It is from the feelings and thoughts emerging from this reflection that generalizations or concepts can be generated, and it is generalizations that allow new situations to be tackled effectively."

These are the 1988 words of Graham Gibbs, the education expert who developed the idea of "reflective learning." Just like with Tanmay Vora above, the key is autonomous conscious control of the learning process. Gibbs cared about experience as a means to learning, but he thought that **it was only when we reflected on this experience that we truly learned something**.

Though this concept may seem abstract, it likely applies to your current learning goal, whatever it is.

Gibbs created his "structured debriefing" process which explained what this reflection actually entailed. It's a *continuous development* cycle for a repeatable experience, i.e., we don't just do it once but repeatedly. It teaches us to reflect and process a particular situation, gaining deeper understanding and arriving at generalizations that enhance learning. Here are the steps:

1. **Describe** – Describe what happened in the situation. Remember the details.
2. **Feelings** – Discuss feelings about the experience.
3. **Evaluation** – How did the experience go?
4. **Analysis** – Make sense of what happened.
5. **Conclusion** – Give two conclusions: a general one and a personal one.
6. **Action Plan** – Sum up everything you need to know and identify how you can improve next time.

Let's take a closer look, with examples. The framework can be applied to minor events you wish to analyze, or more broadly to your own life as a whole. Or both! The following example shows how the framework applies to a broader life situation.

Describe. What happened? Look at when, who, why, where, and how it happened. Be comprehensive but concise, and stick to facts.

Example: *I am on a mandatory training course with an internal team at work because the boss wants everyone to prepare for this new software system. I was enrolled so I could then train my subordinates on the protocol next month. On the first day of the course, the instructor graded my practice report as the worst in the group and loudly criticized me in front of my peers.*

Feelings. What were your thoughts, emotions, beliefs, and values at the time in response to the above? What about others' thoughts?

Example: *I was embarrassed and angry, and thought, "I didn't even want to be on this course. It's mandatory!" I felt this was unfair of the instructor, and I felt picked on. It's shaken me because I'm normally a top performer at work and looked up to by others. The instructor seemed irritated with me.*

Evaluation. Look at the negative and the positive. What worked and what didn't? How did things get resolved—if they did?

Example: *Talking to the instructor after class, I realized that she didn't think she had been unkind and was surprised I was upset. Honestly, my report was not up to scratch, but the instructor could have been gentler. On the other hand, I can at least appreciate that she's an expert in her field and has taken the time to improve my work. Going forward, I'm trying to put my bruised ego aside and genuinely learn to be better.*

Analysis. Use a wider theory or framework to put the event in context and understand it better. Ask WHY questions and see if there is any guidance out there about similar situations. Look for possible alternatives and research various options going forward.

Example: *Sitting with the problem, I've come to realize that my own reaction was more of a defensive response from me, and I wasn't being genuinely attacked by the instructor. I think I was especially touchy that day because deep down I'm a little nervous about the changes happening at the company and insecure about my own value to the team in the future. However, being sulky and unwilling to hear feedback won't help!*

Conclusion. The general conclusion is transferable to other situations in life, whereas the specific one is only applicable to the current situation. Ask yourself: *what have I learned? What could I do better next time? To do better next time, what skills will I need?*

Example: *My general conclusion is that I need to be less complacent and more open to the fact that I can always learn more, even if I consider myself accomplished already. My specific conclusion is that I need to immediately put the instructor's feedback into practice and show her that I can learn and adapt. I think this will go a long way to making me feel more in control.*

Action plan. Summarize everything you know and figure out a way to put this into action right now. How can you *apply* your knowledge and experience? Think about how you can adapt or what you'll do the next time you encounter this problem.

Example: *I will compile a new report incorporating her feedback and ask her to give me private feedback one-on-one when she has a moment. In the future, I'm going to try to be a little less serious about these things and thank people who give me constructive advice, while being aware of my own insecurities putting me on the defensive.*

As you can see from the above example, Gibbs' process outlines the process of **learning about learning**. It's reflective because it asks us to use metacognition and learn about the way we are learning. This is the hallmark of a self-directed, effective learner.

The process doesn't have to be this long and drawn out, though. Here's a simpler, more concrete example:

1. **Describe** – I did well on my music exam, except I failed the sight-reading section.
2. **Feelings** – I'm pretty confused and disappointed; I thought I understood the theory and process.
3. **Evaluation** – Examining my approach, I've probably missed a few important details.
4. **Analysis** – I think I missed these because I joined the class late last year.
5. **Conclusion** – General: pay attention! Specific: Ask for catch-up lessons on this one issue.
6. **Action Plan** – Get in touch with the teacher tomorrow to chat about remedial lessons. Maybe buy that sight-reading book I saw on Amazon. Dedicate some time every evening this month to polishing up this area.

When it all boils down, the ability to reflect on your own learning process is simply the ability to keep asking, what am I doing and is it working? How can I do things better? The thing that reliably interferes with this reflective process is our own ego. We can't reflect on a process if we're unwilling to learn something new about the situation or ourselves!

Now, you may be wondering how exactly this process applies to your specific learning goals. Though it might seem overly general, practicing the skills outlined by Gibbs will improve every aspect of your learning well after you've completed an important exam or achieved this or that goal. In time, these steps may start to become automatic, and you may incorporate them into your thinking naturally.

This is where your learning journal can come in handy. Remember that, according to Gibbs, any experience is an opportunity for learning, provided you reflect on it! For example, let's return to the two questions we began with earlier in the chapter: How have you studied and learned new things in the past, and how well has that worked for you? Specifically, can you think of a time when things didn't go according to plan?

Now, try to use Gibbs' framework to help you conduct a kind of post-mortem on this experience and reflect on it. Work through the steps until you arrive at an action plan that inspires you to **do** something about what you've experienced.

You may notice that going through this process slows you down and forces you to engage more deeply with what is going on in your life, but also what is going on more specifically in your learning journey. It teaches you to be self-directed, self-aware, and a responsible learner. It also helps you make meaning of the things you're learning and make course corrections in your path toward your goal. The next time you are confused, unmotivated, experiencing failure or disappointment, or unclear on your next step, pick up your learning journal and quickly run through Gibb's steps to help find clarity and a clear way forward. Notice how you feel afterwards—isn't it empowering to take charge of your own process this way?

UNDERSTAND COGNITIVE LOAD AND WORKING MEMORY

In his 2014 talk at the Center for Advancing Teaching and Learning at the University of Wisconsin-La Crosse, Bill Cerbin explained a concept you may already be quite familiar with: **you can't overload your brain!**

He calls it "cognitive overload," and it impairs student memory and learning. The brain has natural and inbuilt limits to the amount of new information it can take in. If we don't respect these limits, we may find ourselves frustrated, exhausted, and no better at remembering anyway.

When we talk about learning *effectively* or *efficiently*, what we mean is: we want to find ways to reduce cognitive load while at the same time increasing how much we learn. Now, why do people get overwhelmed when learning something new? Is it:

The speed the teacher covers the material?

The complexity of the material?

The way the information is organized?

Actually, according to Cerbin, what creates overwhelm is two things: our cognitive load and our working memory.

Working memory is what allows us to hold on to a limited amount of brand-new information as we encounter it, for a short period of time. It's like the workspace of our conscious mind. What we ordinarily think of as thinking and processing is really happening in our working memory brain centers.

The trick here is that working memory is actually very limited and can only hold a small of information at a time. Imagine that your working memory is what you can hold in your cupped hands. Anything over and above this quantity just falls out of your grasp—i.e., information that outstrips your working memory will simply not be grasped in any meaningful way.

The metaphor that Cerbin uses is that of a bottle: imagine that our memory is a wine bottle. Your long-term memory storage is the main body of the bottle, but your working memory is the narrower spout— only so much can enter at one time. Before memories can enter long-term memory, they need to be processed through the "bottleneck" of working memory.

Now, cognitive load refers to the "mental resources" needed to accomplish any particular task or process some new information. New tasks carry a bigger load than familiar ones; bigger tasks have greater loads than smaller ones, and complex tasks have a higher load than simple ones.

Cognitive overload occurs when the cognitive load of a task exceeds our working memory's natural limitations. In other words, it's like trying to shove too much into a narrow bottleneck, or struggling to grasp too much in two cupped hands. You'll know you're in cognitive overload when you start making errors, getting confused, feeling overwhelmed or anxious, or even wanting to give up in frustration.

So what can we take from this understanding? Well, obviously: your brain has limits. It's not a machine. There is an *optimal* range of new information it can take in, and beyond that point, learning decreases. But does that mean we are trapped forever to take in new information limited to a few small pieces of information at a time? Luckily, no!

Understanding that our working memory has limits means we can artificially extend these limits. So, your working memory is pretty puny, but you have almost unlimited tools at your disposal to extend that working memory. An easy example: if someone asked you to remember a list of twenty random words, you probably would max out your working memory and do poorly on the task. But by simply writing down the words to retrieve later, you completely ease the cognitive load, since the pen and paper serve as artificial extensions of your own working memory.

So to learn more, we have two choices:

1. Expand our natural working memory
2. Work with tools that help lower our cognitive load

We can achieve much, much more if we focus our efforts on number 2.

In any learning situation, there are three sources of cognitive load that make demands on our limited working memory:

Essential load – the effort you need to learn a task or do something new, on an essential and superficial level.

Generative load – deeper processing to make sense of the new material, including integrating and understanding. This is more than just remembering; it's understanding and comprehending, knowing *why* you do the tasks in the essential load.

Extraneous load – the effort of processing material irrelevant or unrelated to the main task. This could be interruptions, distractions, or poor explanations/teaching material.

If we want to reduce cognitive load, we need to be aware of the different types. Generative load is more difficult, but the payoff is greater because it accompanies greater recall and comprehension, so we don't want to reduce it. But extraneous load is completely unnecessary and needs to be reduced entirely.

The ways to reduce cognitive load will be discussed in later chapters, but for now, it's enough to understand that your brain does, in fact, have limits and that you undermine your learning when you disrespect these limits. In essence, every one of the techniques we will discuss in some way lowers cognitive load, but the most important thing at first is to simply be aware that it's happening, and why.

Tip 1: Respect your limitations and take enough rest

You can squeeze the whole ocean through that bottleneck—if you're patient enough! Similarly, the best learning takes place when we are able to pace ourselves and process new information at a realistic speed. This means taking time to stop, have a break, replenish our cognitive resources, and come back to the task later.

Being fatigued or sleep deprived will make your working memory even smaller than it normally is, so make sure you build in plenty of breaks and get quality sleep every night. Other than that, notice whenever you start to feel overwhelmed or confused and ask if you need to dial things back and take in the new information one bite at a time.

Remember that rushing or forcing more new information that your working memory can handle is just increasing the overload—it's not making it any easier for your brain to process anything.

Tip 2: Condense, chunk, and generalize

At least when information is still new, try to lower its complexity, slow down its delivery, and keep it well organized. It may be a helpful first step to just condense, generalize, and summarize what you need to learn so you can gain an overview. For example, you could skim a text before diving into it. We'll delve into "chunking information" in more detail later on, but this is nothing more than breaking big overwhelming blocks of data into smaller, more manageable chunks.

For example, you could see a giant essay in front of you and break it down into paragraphs, committing only to understanding the main point of each paragraph at a time. Later, you can try to put all these ideas together, but first just extract smaller chunks.

Tip 3: Eliminate extraneous load by cutting away the inessential

This sounds obvious, but many of us deliberately overwhelm ourselves when we try to process too many things at once, especially things that are not essential to our understanding. Cut down on distractions by turning off TV and radio, putting your phone in another room, and making sure nobody is bothering you while you're studying.

Sit somewhere quiet and comfortable with minimal distractions. Make sure that you're not overly tired or hungry, or unconsciously waiting for an upcoming appointment that weakens your attention and focus.

For now, we will simply be aware that we can never learn beyond the limits of our working memory. Knowing this, however, empowers us to find smart ways around these limits without exhausting ourselves or jeopardizing our learning.

GAMIFICATION

Gamification for learning means you incorporate gaming mechanics to boost learning. Gamification is important because it not only enhances learning, it

also increases motivation levels and promotes engagement. When you make things a game, you encourage yourself to explore things in different ways; plus, you boost your motivation. This is why gamification has been used extensively by software designers and marketers—the idea is to create a way of engaging with information that is, for lack of a better word, addictive!

To gamify your learning experience, you can simply learn to include essential game elements into your study routine. Conventionally, technology is seen as a distraction and the opposite of hard work and learning, but we can adjust our mindset and see that gamifying our work with technology is actually a way to leverage our engagement to make us better, more efficient learners.

Gamification improves your problem-solving skills, boosts your critical thinking, helps you sustain attention and motivation, and may even enhance your collaboration with others and your social awareness if you "game" with others. Here are a few golden rules to keep in mind when trying to gamify your own study approach:

1. Make things genuinely *fun*! Endorphins help with recall and learning.
2. The hippocampus plays a big role in memory, and its function is linked to dopamine release and the emotional sensation of reward, so make sure your learning feels *meaningful* to you and connects with you on an emotional level.
3. Remember that the brain is built for *connections*, relationships, and stories, rather than dry and detached facts.

How can you gamify your learning process? You probably already have an intuitive sense of what this might look like, especially if you're a gamer of any kind! Here are some ideas:

Give yourself tiny rewards

Some learning tasks are difficult because the reward is so far off in the distance. You work and work and work and yet you don't feel as though much has changed, and all that results is that you're tired. Change things up by making sure you receive tiny rewards at more regular intervals. These rewards will stimulate the release of neurotransmitters in the brain that boost motivation and strengthen the feeling that the action you've just performed is a good one.

Give yourself points, badges, prizes, or tokens of achievement when you achieve a small step on your path. Not only will this make you feel like you've made progress, but it will also inspire you to race to earn the next one.

For a simple example, imagine you allow yourself to eat one jelly bean per page of challenging text you read. A jelly bean is just a silly thing, and if you really wanted to, you could gobble the whole bag. But by turning it into a game, you set a fun challenge for yourself and see how far you can go.

Set up a progress indicator

Closely related to this technique is to deliberately set up markers that let your brain know it's making progress on its journey. This alone will be perceived as a reward. Though small, this feeling of achievement and actually getting somewhere is highly motivational.

You can set up a "progress bar" for yourself in many ways: have a poster on which you cross out days, challenges, or tasks, or something cumulative where you can watch your daily growth toward a goal, like a jar you add a coin or marble to after each completed task.

Consider creating a collage that represents your goal, and literally draw a line that gets longer and longer the closer you get to that end point. Simply seeing the cumulative effect of your progress encourages you because you don't want to "break your streak" or lose momentum.

Here's one place your learning journal can be put to use. Simply going back to the goals you set for yourself a week or month before and seeing how far you've come gives you a feeling of pride and accomplishment that makes you want to keep going.

Add an element of competition

In keeping with the idea of making learning more collaborative and social, see what you can do to playfully vie against your peers. Naturally, you don't want to take this too far!

When there's a task to be done, you could break into teams or groups and compete against one another. Another way to bring in some competition is to have a "leader board" system where the top performer gets to occupy a special place on a notice board that announces their rank. This not only encourages others to see if they can do better, but it also encourages the reigning champion to keep on their toes.

Create low-stakes challenges

Not everyone responds to competition, time limits, or rewards the same way. Sometimes, and for some subjects, what works best is to have a task where you are trying your very best but without any penalty if you fail or do it wrong.

Low-stakes challenges encourage open minds and creative, out-of-the-box solutions. For example, one particularly fun but beneficial activity is to deliberately choose to do a task as *wrong* as possible. Or challenge yourself to completely immerse in a present problem and follow a bad course of action to its logical conclusion. The game here is that eventually you start seeing a real solution.

Turn things into a story

The most absorbing games are typically those that follow a clear and understandable narrative. You know exactly where you're going and why. You may discover that your interest in a task is greater when you have a strong sense of how your actions fit into a greater narrative context. If you have a particularly stubborn challenge you're facing, conceptualize it as a "boss" at your current level that you have to defeat.

Keep it dynamic and unexpected

The best games are fun, and the worst ones are boring, predictable, and plodding. Bring in an element of surprise into your study. For example, invite a friend to challenge you to an unknown problem, or put a selection of written problems in a bag and randomly draw one from the pile.

To make it more fun, mix in a few genuinely difficult tasks along with some freebies or prizes that allow you to have a reward or bonus. This recreates the addictive feeling of "spinning the wheel" to see the outcome. Only allow yourself to dip into the bag again when you've solved the previous problem correctly.

INTRINSIC MOTIVATION

In reading all the above, you may be wondering if gamification really works—don't people quickly tire of chasing carrots?

Research has suggested (Yeager & Bundick, 2009) that when people learn not simply for external reward but because they genuinely find the activity interesting and gratifying, they are more effective and better at overcoming challenges. Gamification is based on external reward, but it may be that operating out of intrinsic purpose and desire is more effective.

Author Daniel Pink explains how *intrinsic* motivation may be more effective at keeping us engaged in learning in the long run than *extrinsic* motivation. According to him, three key components of internal motivation—mastery, autonomy, and purpose—are what makes it more satisfying and effective than merely being driven to do something because of outside rewards.

Mastery means we keep trying again and again until we gain complete control over a task. We need specific, clear, and demonstrable goals. We need a clear objective to aim for and feedback that helps us adjust along the way.

Autonomy means we get to choose what we do on our learning path (i.e., we are self-directed, as described above). As a self-directed learner, your challenge may be to recognize all the choices available to you and own them.

Purpose means we act with a reason. There is some point to our learning, and it's worthwhile to us personally. Our actions need to feel relevant and important.

Does this mean that gamification is really not a great way to boost our learning? Well, it's not either/or. A great strategy is to use *both*. In a general sense, pay attention to whether your study program is providing you with mastery, autonomy, and purpose, but that doesn't mean you can't also further encourage yourself with gamification tricks in specific moments.

For example, you may have the goal of learning to play the traditional Irish harp, the cláirseach.

Mastery: Every day you set up tasks that allow you to practice, refine your skills, and try again until you perfect certain abilities.

Autonomy: You chose this instrument, and you created your own study goals and schedule. You decided on the pace and tone of your lessons and the favorite pieces you'd practice.

Purpose: Most importantly, you never forget why you're learning the instrument in the first place. You draw on your love of the music and knowing you participate in a proud shared cultural and familial heritage, which deeply satisfies you on a personal level.

However, on a day-to-day level, playing the cláirseach is hard and boring work! You need to do taxing and difficult scales and fingering exercises. So, you use gamification to help you get through some of the slog. For example, you create a little chart on your wall onto which you stick a golden star every time you complete an hour session. Seeing the growing line of stars gives you a temporary boost in flagging motivation.

If you are routinely finding that you need to bully, coerce, beg, or trick yourself into doing learning tasks, it may point to a lack of intrinsic motivation. After all, no flashing smartphone app, sticker, or badge is going to replace your genuine disinterest. If this is you, ask yourself:

Have I given myself enough opportunity to develop real mastery and build competence?

Am I taking full responsibility for my learning journey, or is someone else in control?

Am I energized by a deeper reason for doing any of it?

If you're having difficulty with these questions, then your first task is to resolve them before using the temporary Band-Aid of gamification.

Takeaways:

- The evidence-based scientific facts tell us that our conventional understanding about learning is sometimes wrong. It's a good idea to be clear about the study approaches you've used so far and be honest about how well those are actually serving you. It may be time to try something completely new!
- Self-directed learning is as much about useful methods as it is about attitude, mood, perception, and feeling. It is important to cultivate the right mindset when it comes to learning. A self-directed learner is ideally playful, autonomous, open to experience, flexible, self-accepting, and capable of internal evaluation and motivation. Identify your goals, stay curious, challenge yourself, track your progress, be intrinsically motivated, collaborate with others, and keep a "study journal" to actively reflect on your progress.
- According to Gibbs, it is only when we actively reflect on our experiences that we truly learn. We can use his "structured debriefing process": **describe** the factual situation, describe our **feelings** about it,

evaluate the experience, make an **analysis**, arrive at two **conclusions** (one general, one specific), and formulate an **action plan** for next time.
- The brain has natural and inbuilt limits to the amount of new information it can take in, and we cannot overload it. Long-term memory is the bottle, and short-term memory is the narrow spout. We can lower cognitive load by condensing, limiting distractions, and having enough breaks.
- Gamification means incorporating gaming mechanics into learning to boost motivation and engagement. Remember, though, that internal motivation is ultimately more powerful, so try to include elements of **mastery, autonomy, and purpose** in your learning.

Chapter 2: Just the basics? Reading, Note-Taking, and Writing

We've considered ways to cultivate the optimal learning mindset, and now it's time to put those attitudes to work. In this chapter, we'll explore a big part of what makes up most people's learning: reading. Effective study needs a focused strategy for taking in, processing, and organizing everything you encounter. The first step: understand exactly what you're reading!

SQ3R METHOD

SQ3R is a study method for students who want to improve their overall reading comprehension. It was originally created in 1941 by pioneer of literacy theory Francis P. Robinson, and even though critics at the time believed it was too complex, the aim of the method was to simplify.

If your study relies heavily on written texts and books, you may find it easy to get bogged down in too much complex information. The ability of **the SQ3R study method to help students focus on the most important information** within the learning materials is its strength. By breaking down the task of reading into more manageable steps, the five steps of SQ3R help students get the most out of their reading material and find focus. The SQ3R stands for:

Survey – To get a sense of the material, look over all the chapter headings and subheadings. Skim the paragraphs. This should only take around three to five minutes and prepares your brain for what's coming.

Question – Generate study questions from the content you surveyed. One great way to do this is to look at the subheadings you've skimmed and turn them into questions. For example, "Chirality and mirror transformations" becomes "what is chirality?" and "how does chirality relate to mirror transformations?"

Read – You begin reading the text while answering the chapter questions as well as the self-generated questions you created in step 2.

Recite – Process it out loud using your own words. Reading and reciting should take the most of your time.

Review – Check all of the same headings you identified in step 1 and summarize all the information in your own words. You could also incorporate diagrams and mind maps.

It really is as simple as that. Here's an example:

Let's say you are working your way through some heavy philosophical writings. You're trying to gain a deeper and more sophisticated understanding of the social and cultural events leading up to the French Revolution, and in particular the influence of the writings of the Marquis de Sade and later Mary Wollstonecraft.

You first skim read through everything (i.e., **survey**) and take note of the chapter headings, the various quotes and highlighted sections, and the labels on the images. You get a sense for how long each piece might take to read and notice that two of the works you've chosen are by the same author. You get a feel for what you're getting yourself into, but you don't actually read anything yet.

Out of this skimming, some questions start to bubble up in your mind (i.e., the **question** stage). What are the authors of each of these pieces trying to achieve? Do they agree with each other or are they presenting completely different accounts? What is each one focusing on and are they all equally useful in helping you reach your learning goals? Maybe you start wondering if there are in fact better resources out there, and how you might find them.

Eventually, you sit down to **read** (with or without jelly beans!), but you go slowly this time, section by section. You bear in mind your original questions. As you complete each paragraph or subsection, you pause and ask yourself what the main topic is. You might even decide to jot down a single sentence in the margins that summarizes each paragraph. Your earlier question ("what is each author trying to achieve?") gets answered in due course as you start to tease out their main arguments.

But it doesn't stop here. You keep reading, and the answers you find actually generate more questions. You find yourself noticing links and connections to other parts of the text, as well as to other texts. You start to see bigger emerging themes. You start scribbling down notes, even writing unanswered questions or disagreements in the margins.

When you're done reading, you **recite**. You close the books and take a moment to see if you can rephrase the ideas you've just encountered. Can you recall the information and summarize it in your own words? There's a lot of extraneous material, but what's *the most important* part?

You notice you're still unclear on a few tricky points. You note these but read again. You finally reach the **review** stage and decide you'll make a summary of everything you've read, with only the most important parts condensed and collected into main themes from all the authors. You end up with a single-page outline. Using the SQ3R method, you feel like you understand this material inside out, whereas just a few hours before, it completely boggled your mind!

Is there any concrete scientific evidence that this method really works, though? David R. Carlston found in his 2011 paper in the journal *Teaching of Psychology* that when students used this method, they did in fact retain more information when it came time to take exams. So that means not only does SQ3R help you zoom in on the most essential information, going through the process itself also improves memory formation so that you can recall what you've learned later on.

A 1978 paper in the *Journal of Reading* (Dolores Tadlock) took a closer look at SQ3R and concluded that it was really an example of another model called the *Information Processing Theory of Learning*. Using the method essentially trains you to work better with your brain's information processing systems.

That said, the method doesn't always work. Disadvantages include the fact that it may take time to learn, and at least at first, you need to remember all the steps. It may also be tricky to implement if you're taking online classes, and it's certainly not a good fit for any study that isn't predominantly text-based.

A few hints and tips if you decide to use this method:

- Be deliberate and slow at first. Start with questions and not what you already know. It may seem awkward to start out a process with what you don't know, but resist the temptation to rush ahead and engage with the material without first homing in on what is unclear.
- When you read, do so actively. Imagine the page is talking to you, and talk back. Ask questions, quickly make summaries in your mind every time you finish a paragraph, and constantly compare what you read with the questions you began with.
- Don't rush through the recitation process, as this may be the most important. Remember cognitive load? Your working memory will only be able to process a thin, steady stream of information at one time. Rush this step and you don't give enough time for material to enter the long-term memory.

Remember, finally, that the SQ3R method is actually a cycle and done continuously. You may choose to repeat the cycle more frequently at first rather than read enormous texts and try to slog through the steps that way.

3-2-1 STRATEGY

As we've seen with the SQ3R method, our learning is impacted by the quality of the reading we do, and our reading is impacted by how well we are able to condense, process, and summarize what we encounter on the page.

When summarizing, readers must not only concentrate but actively **engage** with the material on a conceptual level. Think of reading comprehension as the stage when you are converting the written word into a data format that is recognized by your brain so it can be stored properly in your memory.

One simple summarizing tool that can help is the 3-2-1 strategy. It involves summarizing key ideas, rethinking them, and posing a question to reveal uncertainty. Basically, the 3-2-1 strategy is filling out a chart that requires: **three things you found out, two interesting things that made you curious, and one question you still have.**

You could also modify this to end with one thing you can concretely do with what you've learned. Or, if you want to use this frame to encourage reflection of the study process, try listing three things you know, two things you don't know, and one thing you've struggling with. If you quickly do this process before a learning activity as well as after, it gives you a helpful framework to track your progress.

This strategy can also be modified depending on *what* you are studying. For instance, if you are studying the transition from feudalism to the emergence of nation states, you can apply it and write down the following by listing **three** key facts about feudalism, **two** effects of feudalism on the economy, and **one** question you still have about the topic.

If you are more interested in the learning process itself, then your list will tend to focus more on those ideas. It doesn't quite matter how you do it; what's important is that you are engaging with the text, rethinking ideas, and focusing on those that you're most interested in or challenged by.

Let's take a closer look.

If you want to focus on conceptual and analytical learning, find:

Three metaphors or symbols, two things they have in common, and one way they support the overall aim of the text.

Three underlying assumptions of the topic, two common misunderstandings of the topic, and one idea that used to be an assumption but is now seen as a misunderstanding.

Three strengths of the process under study, two styles or forms of that process, and one way it might evolve in the future.

If you want to focus on engagement, debate, or discussion, find:

Three ways you agree, two ways you disagree, and one thing that surprised you.

Three claims someone else is making, two things they disagree with, and one thing you feel they haven't provided evidence for.

If you want to focus on reflection about your learning process, find:

Three things you know about yourself, two flaws you need to work on, and one new thing you've learned about yourself.

Three open-ended questions, two closed questions, and one probing question.

Three ways your study strategy is working, two ways it isn't, and one practical step you can take right now.

And so on. You can also use 3-2-1 for organizing research or research questions, focused reading, or even troubleshooting.

As you can see, there is nothing magical about the numbers three, two, and one. You could put them in any order and focus on any ideas, topics, or themes you wanted to. The usefulness of this technique lies in the fact that it forces autonomous engagement with what you're reading. When we do active reading (or ask questions in the SQ3R method, for example), what we are doing is *processing* the information rather than just passively *absorbing* it.

Because of this method's simplicity, it's great to combine with other study techniques. Here are some ideas, for example:

- You're using the Gibbs model described above to analyze your performance on a math exam. You move through the steps of describe, feelings, evaluation, analysis, etc., but for each step, you look for three separate chunks of information. For example, for the first step of "describe," you find three things that happened in the exam, two things that you were unprepared for, and one thing you feel everyone else also experienced with the exam. Next, for the "feelings" step, you find three feelings you feel now, two feelings you felt before the exam, and one feeling you expect to feel tomorrow.
- You're trying to learn a lot of new vocabulary in a new language, but you're working hard to respect your cognitive limitations and not overload your working memory. So you ask yourself to identify three of the most important words you absolutely need to remember (essential load), two that are more difficult (generative load), and one word or piece of information that you can ignore

(extraneous load). The 3-2-1 method allows you to practically apply this understanding about working memory.

- You're trying to brush up on certain math skills by gamifying your learning process. You create a store of practice problems at easy, medium, and hard difficulty levels. Then as a challenge, you assign yourself three easy, two medium, and one hard task. When you complete these, you give yourself a mini reward. Perhaps, to finish the study session, you invert this and do one easy problem, two medium, and three hard—solve this ultimate challenge and you award yourself a session badge and complete your tasks for the day feeling proud and accomplished.

Some people may find the 3-2-1 method a little vague and wonder how exactly they could apply it to their own situation or study material. But asking these questions is precisely where the benefit lies! The more you autonomously shape and guide your own learning, the better your comprehension, the better your processing, and the better your memory formation and recall. In other words, you'll learn faster.

Here's a great way to start applying the method right now: close this book and see if you can remember three facts about the method just discussed, two things that stuck out to you as most interesting, and one thing you're still not sure about or disagree with.

FRAYER MODEL

Let's return to the example question we had earlier on: "What is chirality?"

When learning concepts, it is likely that you will come across terms that are initially a challenge to comprehend. Understanding and processing what we're reading often comes down to understanding a new concept, but to do that, we need to know the meaning of the *word* itself.

A tool that can help us to analyze words and understand their underlying concepts is something called the Frayer Model. First developed by Dorothy Frayer, Wayne Fredrick, and Herbert Klausmeier in

1969 at the University of Wisconsin, it's a simple but useful way to organize your understanding of new academic terms. It is a four-square graphic organizer that **determines, clarifies,** and **analyzes** word meaning and structure. Doing so helps you really grasp and comprehend the material you're taking in.

First, the word to concentrate on is written in an oval in the center of a page or chart paper. A section of speech is sometimes included in the oval. Surrounding this oval are the four squares of a larger square, and each of these squares is blank except for the following headings:

1. **Definition** – What is the word/concept's meaning?
2. **Characteristics** – What are the specific details/features of the word/concept?
3. **Examples** – Give examples based on the word you're analyzing.
4. **Non-examples** – Things that DO NOT APPLY to the word you're analyzing. This will help in strengthening your understanding of the definition.

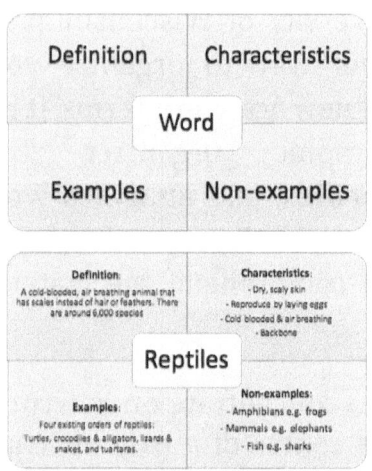

The above is an example (from the www.theconfidenteacher.com).

This tool can be used for almost anything but may work better for things like literature and poetry, or else subjects with plenty of new academic or scientific/technical jargon such as law or biology. You may also discover that analyzing new terms this way gives you fresh insights into its etymology (its origin), its morphology (how it can be changed and adapted to vary its meaning), and its history (how the meaning may have evolved or changed over time). All of this gives you a deeper and richer comprehension on both the word and topic it references.

So, *when* and *how* do you use this tool?

The tool is useful anytime you want to go deeper than plain facts and get a better grasp of the concepts behind certain vocabulary words and terms. Abstract concepts are quite difficult to define, and many of us simply assume we understand a concept, or gloss over it and replace it with more superficial level facts.

For example, "democracy originated with the ancient Greeks" is a fact. It's easy to memorize. You could simply learn these details and regurgitate them on a multiple-choice exam without ever truly understanding what the word "democracy" means on a more abstract level. What the Frayer Model does is slow you down and help you pick apart a concept from all angles so that you can genuinely comprehend its meaning. This way, your learning is deeper and more robust—and so is your memory.

Let's look at an example of how you might use the Frayer Model to break down and grasp a complex concept.

Definition

This is a great starting point, but on its own, it's not enough for true comprehension. Using the dictionary is necessary; ask what the big idea is. For example, let's say the term in the middle of your four squares is "prime number." The definition here is: "a number that is divisible only by itself and the number one."

Essential Characteristics

Let's take the definition a step further. "A prime number is a natural number. Prime numbers cannot be written as the product of two smaller natural numbers. Every natural number greater than 1 is either a prime number or can be factorized as a product of primes that is unique up to their order. Prime numbers must be whole, positive, and always odd, other than two."

These are all essential characteristics about the concept called prime numbers. In fact, in math, prime numbers have one essential and defining characteristic which gets its own new term: primality.

Examples

Here we are in the realm of facts, and we find an instance of the "rules" we discovered in the essential characteristic box. Can we think of a time when these characteristics apply? "The number 5 is prime because it is divisible only by itself and 1, and the only ways of writing it as a product involve 5 itself (1 × 5 or 5 × 1)." More possible prime numbers are: 2, 3, 5, 7, 11.

In this particular example, we can actually find all the examples in a fixed and knowable order!

Non-examples

We understand a concept well when we also understand what it *isn't*. This is a way to draw crystal-clear lines around the concept you're referring to and the concepts you're not. Ask which ideas, concepts, or things expressly do not follow the definition or essential characteristics.

In this example, it could be, "The number 4 is not a prime number because it can be divided by a number other than 1 and itself (2), and its composite (2x2) contains numbers smaller than 4." Also, "The numbers -2 and 0.75 are not prime because they are negative and not whole, respectively."

You can use the Frayer Model for any concept, from complex to simple. The above example is very concrete, but you may find yourself dealing with higher order, vaguer, and "fuzzier" concepts, like this:

"Power."

Definition: The capacity to influence people or things; the ability or capacity to do something

Characteristics: Power can be intellectual, physical, chemical; it can be emotional or relational; learned or inborn; natural or forced, etc.

Examples: A president, electricity, currency, a tidal wave, a programming language, blackmail

Non-examples: a newborn baby, a broken elevator, a crumb, an incarcerated criminal

As you can see with the above example, this technique can also be used to expand on abstract concepts, and even start to explore some hidden depths, new questions, or alternatives framings. For example, is it really true that a newborn baby has no power? Doesn't it have the power to keep everyone else up all night? Isn't there immense power in its ability to scream the house down, or to emotionally command all the attention in a room?

By using the Frayer Model, you can explore all the depths, nooks, and crannies in a concept's definition—and in doing so have a much more sophisticated understanding of what you're learning.

SEMANTIC FEATURE ANALYSIS

It's no exaggeration to say that the more finely you master the art of reading and language, the better your comprehension and memory, i.e., the more effective you are at learning.

Semantic Feature Analysis is another method that helps you get a good grip on the terms you may encounter when learning something new. It uses a grid to aid students in exploring the *relationships* between terms and the features those terms possess. It allows you to find links, make predictions, and master important concepts while actively completing the grid and examining its outcomes.

Creating a semantic feature analysis is simple:

1. Identify concepts and/or terms to be learned and the features of these concepts that can be used to compare them.

2. Create a chart that lists the concepts down the left-hand side and the features across the top.

3. Consider each feature in turn and decide whether the concept exemplifies that feature (mark with +) or does not exemplify that feature (mark with -).

4. Use the chart to explore the concepts further, generate questions, and conduct research.

A sample chart will make this clear:

insects \ features	6 legs	3 body parts	has wings	lays eggs	bites	stings
bees	+	+	+	+	-	+
ants	+	+	-	+	?	-
mosquitoes	+	+	+	+	+	-
wasps	+	+	+	+	-	+
cricket	+	+	-	+	-	-

In the same way that using examples and counterexamples helps you better grasp a concept, comparing and contrasting the features of certain concepts helps you give clear definition to their essential characteristics.

At a glance of the table above, for example, you can see that all your chosen insects have three things in common: six legs, three body parts, and the ability to lay eggs. You also notice other intriguing patterns: the insects that don't sting, for example, bite, and vice versa, although the cricket does neither. You also see that there is some information you don't have (do ants bite?), and this leads you down another path, i.e., that the features may change according to how you subdivide certain concepts (some ants do, others don't).

While this may seem a little complicated at first, a semantic feature analysis grid actually helps you condense enormous amounts of information into one place. You would have to create a long essay or several paragraphs to capture the many relationships and emerging patterns in writing alone. By exploring interconnected relationships between terms, you gain a deeper understanding of those terms. This allows you to make pretty robust predictions and use any "rules" you find to creatively generate your own examples.

The technique can also be used for reflection or to chart your progress. Dr. Mimi Miller and Nancy Veatch wrote a book called *Literacy in Context (LinC): Choosing Instructional Strategies to Teach Reading in Content Areas for Students Grades 5-12*, where they discuss this tool, explaining that, "Semantic Feature Analysis can be used before, during, and after instruction. Before beginning the reading of a passage, the teacher might introduce the terms and find out what students already know. The initial "+" and "-" marks can be written in one color. Then, during or after reading a section of text, students can come back to the chart and revisit their evaluation of the features. After reconsidering, some might be changed from "-" to "+," and vice-versa. These new, revised marks can be made in a different color."

Why not combine such a chart with the SQ3R model described above? During the review or recital phase, you could condense what you know into a chart.

It may take a few tries to master this approach, so don't worry if it seems clunky at first. Here are some tips:

- Start out with less abstract, more concrete ideas first, and try to compare only a few concepts across a limited number of features so your grid doesn't get too big and complicated.
- For "features," choose any traits, characteristics, or properties of the concepts you've chosen. If you draw your grid on a big piece of paper, leave some space below and to the right to add more information if necessary.

- Move down the grid going concept by concept and ask yourself a question for each cell. For example, "How many body parts do wasps have?" or, "Do mosquitos sting or bite?" Don't rush. If you're unsure, just put a question mark—knowing what you *don't* know has its own value!
- Once the grid is complete, you should be able to start seeing broad patterns. Is anything surprising or unexpected? Which concepts are most different and most alike? Do you notice anything interesting, such as two features being mutually exclusive (i.e., a concept always possesses either one feature or the other, never both)? Can you make any predictions about how another concept may perform on the grid?

Naturally, the example with insects is a pretty simple one, but when you use this approach for topics that you are genuinely less familiar with, its value becomes clearer.

That said, the approach is not universally appropriate for every learning task. Use it for organizing reading materials where you need to compare and contrast topics (especially more than two) or when you need to organize different classifications. It can be combined somewhat with the Frayer technique above, in that you can compare two or more *terms* to see how they differ and how they are similar.

For example, you may be a little unclear on the difference between the terms Alzheimer's disease, dementia, neurodegenerative disease, and cognitive decline. There is some overlap, but the terms are distinct, and a semantics feature analysis will let you clearly mark out what the differences and commonalities are.

Give this approach a skip if you're only tackling two concepts, or if you're dealing with something that isn't easy to break down into features. The technique seems to work best for concepts that are not too concrete, not too abstract. If you find that you draw up a grid and it only spurs more questions than it answers, your concepts may be too high-level to be accurately captured. Go back to the drawing board to break them down into simpler concepts, or else reconsider whether you need a different approach entirely.

NOVEL NOTETAKING STRATEGIES

We've discussed four effective methods to help you shape, organize, and take control of your *reading* process, but all of this is incomplete without a way to properly *record* what you've learned. This is where notetaking comes in. **When learning new concepts, taking good notes is one of the most effective ways to remember (and understand) what you're learning. Better notes will help you remember concepts, develop useful learning skills, and comprehend a subject.**

Here are some popular and effective notetaking strategies that can help you:

1. Cornell Method
2. Mapping Method
3. The Outlining Method
4. The Charting Method
5. The Sentence Method

On important point—the effectiveness of your notes has nothing to do with how long they are or how neatly written. Rather, what matters is how they're *organized*. Even the neatest, tidiest, and nicest looking notes will be useless if they are organized poorly and mean nothing to you personally. Likewise, a small, scruffy half page with a few pertinent notes can do more to help your learning than a whole study manual.

Whichever method you end up using, good notes have a few things in common:

- You make them yourself, in your own words
- They arise from *active* listening and reading
- They show deeper meanings, patterns, and connections, not just facts
- They simplify things and help you relax, rather than make your life more complicated

Let's take a closer look, with some examples.

The Cornell Method

Notes are summarized neatly, pulling out all the key concepts and giving you something easy to review. Here's how you do it.

First, divide the page into three parts: a two or three inch margin on the left side, the so-called **cue section**; a two inch **summary**

section on the bottom; and the remainder of the paper in the middle, the **in-class notes section.**

During a lecture or while reading, scribble down notes in the main section. These could include questions, insights, little diagrams, and paraphrased summaries. Later, when you're out of class, use the cue section on the left to write down prompts to help you remember the main points from the notes you've just taken.

For example, write down a key vocabulary word or summarizing statement that, when you read it, will help jog your memory for the main information—for example, "historical background" or "the chloroplast's structure" or "what was Locke's rebuttal?"

Finally, in the summary section on the bottom, you condense the notes you've taken that day into a paragraph that contains the main ideas. Do this for each and every page. Going back to review, you now have a usable summary as well as prompts that help you remember the broader themes and ideas—invaluable when you're revising!

The Mapping Method

This is a more visual technique and will help you quickly grasp relationships between concepts. You may already be familiar with mind maps—the concept here is the same. While in class, start with a big bubble with the lesson's theme written in the middle. Then, in branches stemming from that main theme, start to draw subtopics, with a new bubble for each "sub header."

Draw lines off these sub headers to add bullet point–style notes, branching off further and further for each subpoint. You might end up with something that looks a little like a branching, upside-down tree or an octopus!

While the Cornell method would work great for, say, a literature class where certain themes were being covered, or in a history class where a linear narrative was being explored, the mapping method is more about charting the relationship between ideas. You could use it, for example, to show a sequence of events (for example, the stages of the Krebs cycle in photosynthesis, or steps in a clinical trial) or outline a decision-making process or historical procedure.

The Outlining Method

If you were trying to compile an essay or analyze an article to extract its underlying structure, you could use this method. Using bullet points and subheadings, you focus on a piece's structure, keeping things properly organized. This looks no more complicated that writing a subheading (for example, "stages of the water carbon cycle") and then jotting down indented bullet points underneath that to briefly list points that fall under that heading.

In fact, this is the primary form this book has taken! This is the style most students default to without thinking about it, and it certainly makes intuitive sense.

The Charting Method

Divide a page into category columns. Now, you can organize and sort the facts you hear/read/encounter into this chart to better understand their relationships. This is not unlike the semantic charting we explored above. For example, you might have three columns: claims of XYZ theorist, evidence they give for the claims, arguments against their claims.

Now, as you read, you may encounter a jumble of facts that fall into either of these categories, perhaps more than one. When you encounter a fact about research and studies done to support the claims, you note it down in the second column, and so on. You may purposely ignore information that isn't relevant to your columns, and in this way, sift through information so that you separate out key ideas. In the end, you have all the relevant info sorted into piles you can then summarize.

The Sentence Method

This is simple: write down each topic as a sentence. Let's say your lecturer is talking about something. You listen carefully, paraphrase what they've just said in your own words, then quickly jot down the sentence.

Though this is the easiest and most straightforward method, it lacks some of the structure of the other approaches. On the other hand, it's flexible and will help if you simply need to get down as much as you hear as quickly as possible.

Every new point gets a new sentence. Try using shorthand and symbols to make writing faster—for example "w/" for "with," two forward slashes (//) to denote "in contrast" or "however," and a giant letter C with the number 18 inside it to indicate "the 18th century."

If you're wondering which of the above is the best method, well, they are *all* effective—what matters is how well they match the learning task at hand. There's nothing to stop you from combining methods, either. You could use a simple sentence method, but when a sub section appears to contain hierarchical information, you could quickly switch to a mapping method to create a useful diagram.

The Cornell method is a firm favorite because it can easily contain all the others and is seemingly applicable for any lecture type. However, if you're not taking notes in an actual spoken lecture, you may find one of the other, more visual methods makes more sense.

Finally, remember that as a self-directed learner, it's your prerogative to see if you'd like to create your own hybrid notetaking strategy!

R.A.F.T.

Before concluding our chapter on notetaking and reading, we'll consider an often-overlooked learning strategy: writing. "Writing to learn" is easily discounted because it feels like a lot of hard work for not much benefit. In truth, feeling uncomfortable with long-form writing can sometimes hint at a less than perfect understanding of the material at hand. After all, this is why so many exam questions are based on essay writing: it's only during the act of compiling a logical, coherent piece of writing that a person demonstrates their true understanding of the concept.

We can use writing as a skill to fine-tune our learning process—that is, if we're deliberate and organized about it.

The RAFT technique promotes creative thinking and helps you think about what you've read in novel ways. The acronym RAFT stands for the following prompts:

Role – Who is the writer and what is their role?

Audience – To whom are you writing?

Format – Are you writing to persuade, entertain, inform, or describe? Something else?

Topic – What are you writing about?

Using RAFT, you zoom out a little and pay attention to the *purpose and function* of any text. You can do this from a reader's perspective, too, but it is often so much more insightful to create a piece from scratch yourself, as the author. If you find writing tedious, it may be because you lack clarity on any of the four aspects outlined above; for example, you are not really certain what your role is; you don't know who the intended audience is; you're confused on the style, tone, or format; or you simply don't have a good grasp on the material itself.

The idea with writing to learn is that **the process of communicating something helps you better understand it from the inside**. In Chapter 4, we'll be taking a closer look at how "teaching" someone else can be like shining a light on gaps in your own understanding. Similarly, switching perspectives and putting yourself in the author's shoes gives you insights and perspectives you might not have accessed as the more passive reader.

Here are some examples for how to use RAFT.

Let's say you are preparing for an exam where a substantial portion of the marks come from an essay question. So, you practice ahead of time and write mock essays on topics you've chosen yourself. You start the process with RAFT. For example, on an essay question that asks you to compare and contrast the different clinical approaches for managing and treating diabetes, you write the following:

Role – Persuader, educator

Audience – A peer with some medical knowledge, but not in this exact area

Format – Structured, formal essay with logical argument ending in persuasive conclusion

Topic – Two clinical approaches for diabetes management, compared

It may seem simple, but this straightforward outline actually helps you catch any major issues in understanding *before* you start writing. You now have some standards against which to compare your essay. Are you correctly addressing the audience? Are you making a persuasive argument? The outline lets you know when you've strayed away from the essay's main goal.

You can use RAFT for your own personal study, too. One amazing exercise to do is to create your own essays any time you want to *consolidate and summarize* your learning. You may be surprised at just how clearly things come into focus for you when you take the time to create a coherent flow of text that argues a single, clearly defined point.

In today's hyper-distracted and fragmented online learning landscape, where multimedia continually presents a jumbled and many-sided view on a topic, a simple essay can be a powerful way to discipline your thought. Writing can teach you to delineate an argument step by step, with evidence, in a consistent format that makes sense for your topic.

In this case, your RAFT outline may look like this:

Role – Summarizer

Audience – Self

Format – Reviewing, consolidating essay for revision

Topic – Five key factors that led to the First World War

Sitting down to compile an essay after you've done plenty of reading can not only help you focus and summarize, it can boost your memory. Things that we write down for ourselves tend to have a more concrete place in our minds and tend to be remembered more vividly. So, as you're writing, take the time to paraphrase in your own words. If you like, you may even get some benefit from literally writing your essay using pen and paper. Engaging your sensorimotor skills this way gives you a concrete set of associations to return to later when you're trying to recall the material.

Writing to learn is not appropriate for every student and every topic. It works well for topics where your own critical analysis is important, such as sociology, psychology, literature, politics, philosophy, art, history, or anthropology. It works less well for topics that are more "objective," such as the sciences or those that are more technical and concrete, such as playing an instrument or learning a language.

However, even with these subjects, you can still deepen your understanding by compiling a kind of "essay" that encapsulates and summarizes either your learning process or the material you've learned. For example, you can use colorful PowerPoint presentations, write a speech, or even compile a full lesson where you teach a hypothetical student what you know. In this case, you can still use RAFT and take care to direct your efforts to a specific audience, for a specific goal, in a specific way.

As with all the techniques discussed in this book, the technique itself is not the be-all-end-all, but rather it's important *how* we use each technique. RAFT can help you:

- **Troubleshoot** – Identify areas of misunderstanding or gaps in your knowledge (hint: it's always difficult to write about something you only half understand!).
- **Review** – Synthesize everything you've learned so far and compile a useful written summary for yourself. Both writing and re-reading this

summary make excellent retrieval practice.
- **Organize** – If you have a lot of material, you can gain a better grasp of things by separating out topics and focusing on just one argument/narrative at a time.
- **Expand** – Writing can be creative, too. If you explore two conflicting concepts, for example, you can use an essay to devise your own unique synthesis of the two or a completely new third topic. You can also make predictions, offer your own analysis, or put forward your own arguments, thus enhancing your deep learning skills.

If you have struggled to imagine how RAFT (or writing in general) can benefit your learning journey, don't worry; you may gain insight simply by asking yourself the question: **what is the purpose of this text?** Whether the text is your own or written by others, you immediately gain clarity and focus when you can understand the purpose and function of any text you're engaging with.

Takeaways:

- Reading, writing, and notetaking are likely to be key skills in your learning journey. The SQ3R technique helps you identify the most important parts of anything you read: follow the steps of survey, question, read, recite, and review to help you break more complex texts down into manageable chunks. Repeat the process as a continuous cycle.
- One simple summarizing tool that can help you engage with material is the 3-2-1 strategy. It involves summarizing key ideas, rethinking them, and posing a question to reveal uncertainty. List three things you found out, two interesting things that made you curious, and one question you still have. This helps you process rather than just passively absorb information.
- A tool that can help us analyze difficult new academic terms and understand their underlying concepts is something called the Frayer Model. Create a simple four-square chart that outlines a word's **definition**, c**haracteristics**, **examples,** and **non-examples** to help you fine-tune your understanding.

- Semantic Feature Analysis is another method that helps you get a good grip on new terms and uses a grid to explore the *relationships* between terms and the features those terms possess. Create a grid with concepts along the side and features along the top to compare and contrast their characteristics. This may allow you to make predictions or find patterns.
- Better notes will help you remember concepts, develop useful learning skills, and better comprehend a subject. There are several useful notetaking strategies to experiment with: the Cornell method, the mapping method, the outlining method, the charting method, and the sentence method—or a combination of these.
- Use "writing to learn" by writing essays according to RAFT prompts, which help you understand the purpose and function of a text. **R**ole: Who is the writer and what is their role? **A**udience: To whom are you writing? **F**ormat: Are you writing to persuade, entertain, inform, or describe? Something else? **T**opic: What are you writing about?

Chapter 3: Remember ANYTHING

RETRIEVAL PRACTICE

Have you ever felt like you studied like crazy for an exam, only to find that when it came down to remembering things on the day, your mind went blank? This could be because when you were studying, you were in fact *practicing the wrong thing*.

Retrieval involves recalling facts, concepts, or events from memory.

Simply put, when we do retrieval practice, what we are practicing is this act of remembering. This is what matters since this is the behavior we most want to master and replicate.

The act of retrieving something from your memory strengthens the connections that hold it there, making it more likely that you'll remember it again. The research has repeatedly found that retrieval practice outperforms more common strategies like repeated studying, which often entails just reading and re-reading notes. It remains one of the best-studied and well-supported learning strategies.

Often, students think they have poor memories when in fact what is happening is that they are not studying in a way that actually supports the way their brain makes memories. Luckily, it's not difficult to shift your practice so that you are *rehearsing retrieval*.

There are numerous ways to incorporate retrieval practice into your classroom, and you may even find the process is easier and more satisfying than simply running over notes.

Here are some examples of how retrieval practice can be used:

- Fill out **practice tests**. You can do these after each session or find mock tests that help you prepare for a main exam. The goal is that you never face a question in a real exam that is completely unfamiliar to you!

- If no practice tests are available, **create your own questions** and answer them. Constantly ask how questions may be framed, and practice *how* you will answer them.
- Make your own set of **flashcards** to test your knowledge of the terms' definitions. When you have mastered a card, get rid of it and keep focusing on the more difficult ones (i.e., don't keep practicing how to answer questions you already find easy!).
- **Dump your thoughts** and write down everything you know and remember from the previous lesson before moving on to the next. You could start every study session with a recap of the last session. This warms you up but also gives you hints about your strategy's effectiveness and where you still need to work.
- **Feedback**. Check to see if the information you've retrieved is correct. Check your notes after you've answered a question to make sure you're right. The last thing you want to do is practice answering questions in the wrong way. Don't worry if you keep messing up; there is value in

asking *why* you make mistakes, then drilling the correct approach.
- For critical thinking questions, make **concept maps**. Here, you are practicing an abstract way of thinking, and rehearsing the process of organizing your thoughts no matter what they are.
- **Summaries.** Sometimes your material isn't geared to right or wrong answers, but rather to quality depth analysis. After every section, jot down everything you can remember without consulting the text. You can use the 3-2-1 strategy, create a semantic feature analysis, or make a mind map.

Whatever you do, watch out that you are not just mindlessly following a rut of reading and re-reading. You may *feel* that you are getting somewhere with this approach, but it is an illusion, and one brought on by familiarity and not true mastery. If the first time you ever retrieve new material from your memory is in the exam, then you're putting yourself at a disadvantage!

Structure your study sessions so that the bulk of your time is spent restructuring knowledge from your memory. It may seem like it makes sense to focus on putting information *into* your memory, but your brain doesn't work like that. Instead, the more you practice taking a piece of information *out of* your memory, the stronger it becomes.

Of course, you need to be familiar with the material to start with before you can practice retrieval, but don't get stuck on organizing and tweaking material and then forget about retrieval practice.

Reading, processing, and organizing—these help you understand material.

Digging things out of your memory again and again—this is what strengthens long-term memory.

In essence, practice what you want to become good at. If you want to be good at recalling the right information at the right time, then practice that! Your memory doesn't get better when it gets fuller or larger, it gets better when it gets *stronger*, just like an athlete gets better when they can strengthen their muscles.

For example, as you read through information and make notes, regularly pause, close the book, look away, and try to recall what you've just read. Or ask yourself a few questions at the end of every study session so that you are not just learning to take information in, but also learning to generate it on command. You not only exercise your memory, but give yourself an opportunity to self-correct because the mini-quiz acts as feedback.

Here are a few more tips and tricks to make retrieval a bigger part of your study strategy:

- Practice in short bursts. It's almost always better to have more instances of retrieval of small bits of information than it is to have fewer retrievals of huge chunks of data (it's easier, too!).
- Actively engage with what you produce when you recall. Look at your answers and responses as a teacher would and try to see what, if anything, is going wrong. Then use this to inform your next attempt at learning. For example, if you constantly misremember a date, it may be time for a cleaver mnemonic or a few rounds of drilling before you do retrieval practice again.

- Pay attention to the *format* of your retrieval. If you're practicing for a written exam, focus on written retrieval. But that doesn't mean you can't strengthen a memory by retrieving it orally or just visualizing it in your mind's eye.
- If you notice that you're getting bored with reading and reviewing your same old notes, it might be a sign that you're not properly engaged and need to do more retrieval practice.
- Depending on your learning goals, you might want to practice a few "canned" answers—getting familiar with particular wording to address a particular question. For example, drill the best way to present a physics problem, making sure that you practice including the units, underlining your final answer, and jotting down the given information and variables on the left-hand side. This will keep you organized and make you feel more confident.
- Don't worry if retrieval feels difficult. It's supposed to! The fact that you're

struggling is a sign that your memory muscle is growing stronger.

The next time you sit down to do a study session, look at every presentation slide, note, mind map, article, etc. and try to actively convert it into an activity that you can do to test your memory. Challenge yourself to recreate that table, mind map, or diagram from memory. Look at the headings in an article and convert them to questions, then answer that question, marking it as though you were a teacher checking for full comprehension. Finally, you may even find it helps to give your own lectures or presentations, or explain material to a study companion to not only ensure you grasp the deeper meaning, but that you can recall it on the fly.

INTERLEAVING

Interleaving is a learning technique that involves combining different topics or types of practice to make learning easier. Interleaving is another well-resourced learning strategy, and studies find that interleaving results in improved retention of new information, faster acquisition of new skills, and improved mastery of existing abilities.

Interleaving can be seen in the case of language learning, where someone learning new vocabulary words can mix words from different topics together rather than learning only words from one topic at a time. For instance, if we're learning 3 skills A, B, and C, we may learn them using this pattern AAAABBBBCCCC (conventionally called "block practice"). If we apply interleaving, however, we mix the skills up and go for ABCABCABC or even a more random combination of BBACBABCCA and so on.

Studies show that this approach improves the brain's ability to discriminate and strengthens memory associations. A 2015 study by Rohrer et al., for example, found impressive differences between children who had been taught math using block practice versus interleaving. The block practice group did twenty-five percent better, whereas the interleaving group did a whopping seventy-six percent!

Block practice is very common. We could argue that the fact that we have dedicated periods for each subject in school is the biggest example of block practice—all physics in one block, then all English, then all history. However, today, educational researchers and psychologists are finding evidence that this is not the most effective way to present information to the brain, and that interleaved practice may be better. This applies to all subjects, even things like sports, languages, and music. One interesting finding is that the benefits of interleaving actually grow more pronounced over time, meaning that the gains made are more lasting than with block practice.

In blocking, you learn particular solutions by rote so that when a different problem comes along, you're caught off guard and stumble. With interleaving, your brain is on its toes and constantly looking for patterns and solutions that fit the problem. With blocking, you already know what *kind* of solution you're supposed to be giving, and so you become a little lazy. After all, nothing in the real world resembles blocked practice. The human brain evolved in a complex world of *mixed* tasks. On the other hand, many people find interleaving difficult because it requires a little more planning and effort.

Here are some examples for how you can use interleaving in your overall study strategy. Note how in the following examples, there are several different ways to create each "unit" or skill. Even though the subject remains the same, there are many options on how to vary practice and keep the brain on its toes!

- **Vary the kinds of problem/skills.** In studying for a math exam, you don't practice hour-long blocks of just one type of problem solving (say, quadratic equations). Instead, you give yourself ten minutes to practice quadratic equations and then switch to some mixed trigonometry problems before moving on to a graph question, and starting again at quadratic equations.
- **Vary the way the same problem is solved.** Alternatively, since you want to focus on the trigonometry problems, you find several different types of practice questions and then create your own mock exam where you mix these all up. Instead of doing the same strategy over and over, you teach yourself to look at each problem afresh and ask, what's the best way to

solve this? Note how this has elements of retrieval practice.
- **Vary the level at which you tackle the problem.** Focus again on trigonometry problems but spend some of your time making notes and learning, some of your time solving and grading problems, some of your time reflecting on your progress and trouble areas, and some of your time creating summaries that condense what you've learned.

As you can see, interleaving is very flexible, but it all comes down to **creating variety in how you learn.** What you don't want is to let your brain be lulled into a false sense of security because it is stuck in a predictable routine.

For example, there may be five different ways or techniques to solve quadratic equations. Your math textbook may group these, explaining each approach and then offering a selection of problems that illustrate only that technique. Practicing these questions will help rehearse that skill, but what it won't do is teach you *how to recognize when to use that skill*. So, when you're in an exam and staring at a page of different quadratic equations, you have little idea how to progress because you have not been given any prompts.

If you've practiced with interleaving and retrieval, then you have actually rehearsed the series of questions in your head that make you say, "What kind of problem am I looking at? What am I being asked to do here?" Not only will you do better in the exam, but you actually will understand the problem on a deeper level than someone who has merely learned these separate skills in isolation, never quite seeing how they connect.

However, there's one important caveat: you can't just dive in with interleaved practice. Unless what you're learning is a very simple sequence of motor skills, **you'll need to have some basic familiarity with the topic to begin with**. If you don't, interleaved practice can confuse you and leave you worse off. You'll know this applies to you if you're still shaky using even one technique or piece of data, let alone combine it with others. In this case, you'll need to make sure you're proficient with each unit before you start mixing them up.

For example, if you're learning the guitar from scratch, you really will need to practice individual skills such as scales and chords in batches first. Only after you're reasonably comfortable can you start mixing chords and scales into one lesson. A more proficient student can start an hour-long lesson with some scales, then move on to chords, then practice a few set pieces, go back to scales and chords, and finish with some improvised playing and hand-strengthening exercises. But a true beginner will probably spend that entire hour learning just one scale!

This phenomenon has been termed the "expertise reversal" and refers to the fact that what works for beginners may not be what works for more expert practitioners. Or, in this case, the high variability created by interleaving is more beneficial for more experienced learners than beginners (Kalyuga, 2009).

How do you know if interleaving is right for you? It depends on the level of your current mastery, as well as the subject at hand. The easiest thing to do is simply test it out. Try interleaved practice for a few days and then reflect on your learning process.

Do you feel overwhelmed and confused? Or do you feel comfortably challenged and able to switch tasks without getting disoriented?

Continue with interleaving if you find it is improving your overall recall. But even if interleaving practice isn't appropriate, it doesn't mean it can't be in the future when your skills are more developed.

CHUNKING

Chunking is, like the name suggests, the process of dividing a bigger whole into smaller and more manageable data "chunks." We briefly mentioned chunking when referring to the natural limits of the brain's short-term memory, and indeed chunking is the main trick to getting around these limitations.

Could you remember one hundred random letters in order? Sounds impossible, but read the next sentence. Individual letters have been "chunked" together to form words and sentences, including the one you're reading right now. It would take you almost no time to remember and perfectly reproduce that sentence, even though it contains 102 bits of information (letters) in order. That's the magic of chunking!

Learning everything at once is impossible because our working memory can only hold about seven items of information at a time. But we have a lot of leeway in how we organize those chunks.

A good way to learn is to break down the skill into manageable chunks and master them one at a time until the act becomes automatic. **Not only does chunking keep us organized, it lowers our cognitive load and makes it so that we spend far less cognitive power to remember far more.**

George Miller was the first to introduce the world to the idea that the short-term memory can only manage seven pieces of information. His 1956 experiments and subsequent paper *The Magical Number Seven, Plus or Minus Two: Some Limits on Our Capacity for Processing Information* still influence how we think of learning today.

In 1980, K. Anders Ericsson did some experiments that further confirmed this: they asked students to recite back strings of numbers in order and found that after around seven, their memory started to tap out. The fascinating thing was, after almost two years of training and practice, these students actually ended up learning to memorize sequences up to eighty digits long! They had average IQs and normal memories like you or me. How did they do it? Chunking.

Some may disagree on this exact number, but in fact it doesn't matter exactly how many pieces of data you can manage at one time (there may be contextual or individual differences). What matters is that you understand that your brain has *limits*, and you organize the information in such a way that those limits are managed.

There are three main ways to use chunking to minimize these limits:

- grouping (separating similar items into groups)
- patterns (finding redundancy in information, identifying repeated laws or rules)
- organizing (dividing a group into multiple categories based on meaning)

Chunks give information meaning and context, help lower cognitive load, and improve memory. In fact, your brain already does chunking—if you have ever learned or remembered anything, it's because at some point, you chunked all the separate data bits and skills and mastered them singly first.

To apply chunking more deliberately, here is the basic procedure:

1. Take a look at everything you need to learn or memorize.
2. Use **grouping, patterns, or organizing** to condense this into smaller, simpler chunks (make sure you are connecting the chunks to something you already know, or make them meaningful and contextual somehow).
3. Once you've created chunks, focus on only one chunk at a time.
4. Make consistent time for practice, drilling, and memorizing.

One question is how big or small to make chunks. Too small and each unit becomes boring and repetitive. Too big and you may still find the task too difficult. A little trial and error will help you find the sweet spot. After you master each chunk, remember to consider how that chunk fits into the bigger picture, or the main skill you're trying to master. Keep being an active learner and keep tabs on how you are progressing.

Just remember that your short-term memory will work how it works; it's up to you how you *organize* the information to make it easier or harder for your brain to do what it does. Let's take a look at some examples to make things clearer.

Imagine you have to remember the phone number 084 3722 1239.

There are eleven digits here, and therefore eleven pieces of information. Using George Miller's insight, this simple phone number would already tax the short-term memory. But there are ways to reduce that number. For example, the dialing code or prefix 084 might be the same as your own, so that's easy to remember and is now grouped into one chunk.

Remembering the 3 and the 7 will take effort, but that 22 in the middle is just a repeat and can be condensed down into "double 2," which is now one piece of data, not two. Similarly, 1239 can be reduced from four pieces of data to two when we notice the pattern of 123 that ends in 9.

So, this reduces the total pieces of information from eleven to around six—far more manageable for your short-term memory! Notice as well that simply organizing the number as 084 3722 1239 rather than 08437221239 puts the data into three groups. If you know the general format for the number and how many numbers there are, this, too, helps recall.

When you use chunking, the mental effort your brain makes is the same or lower, but the actual workload is greater. It doesn't matter how you chunk, only that overall, you're reducing the mental workload in this way.

Another example is to remember items on your shopping list by grouping them according to type (vegetables, cleaning products, treats) or according to the meal you hope to make with those ingredients. Using mnemonics (where the letters in a word each stand for another word) is also a way of chunking, since ultimately you only have to remember that one word.

If you had to memorize a series of steps in a biological process, you could use chunking to break the process down into a series of mini processes. If you're learning about oxidative phosphorylation, a complex process, you could break down the procedure according to each enzyme involved and separately learn its function. What's important with this kind of chunking, however, is that you also memorize the way all the chunks fit back together again!

In this example, you could create a mini narrative that maps onto something else in the world you already understand. (For example, a soap opera, where each enzyme represents a character, and their biochemical functions form the events of the story. Let's say the ATP molecule produced at the end is the lovechild and the culmination of a dramatic story!) This will help you keep everything in order without expending much more mental energy.

LEARN BY MAKING ASSOCIATIONS

When we work *with* rather than *against* our brain's natural inbuilt tendencies, we can make the most of our learning. If the brain likes narratives, analogies, and information presented in short, manageable chunks, then shaping our learning this way will make it easier for our brains to do what they do best.

One thing the human brain is especially well suited to is making associations. **Deliberately forming associations to boost our memory and deepen our understanding also makes learning a lot more fun and engaging. Association is simply the process of connecting new information to what we already know.**

We might tie what we want to remember to something we already remember to make it easier to recall. This is because we piggyback one on the other—when we recall one, we can't help but recall the other.

An example of association is F, A, C, and E, which are treble clef spaces in music. As we saw in the previous section on chunking, a random series of letters is going to be hard to memorize because it simply doesn't *mean* anything. But join them together to form a word, and making the association between a "face" and the treble clef spaces makes it far easier to recall.

There are two types of associations: the **unintentional** (conditioned learning) and **intentional** (where you choose which associations are the most powerful cues, putting yourself in charge of your own learning). The classic example of an unintentional association is the experiment with Pavlov's dogs, who soon learned to associate the ringing of a bell with the arrival of food, because the two events were paired together. The association formed was so strong that simply hearing the ringing bell was enough to produce a response—salivation.

Using intentional associations can be just as powerful, or more so. Both approaches work because they are aligned with the way the brain stores memories.

Imagine that memories are filed away in a web. Each node is a remembered piece of data, but it is connected to several other nodes in the network. When you pull on one node, you can't help but pull on other associated nodes. For example, when you recall an old school friend, you seem to automatically recall the house you lived in at that time, the hairstyle you had at that age, the smell of your school classroom, and a particular event that happened there. This is because all these events form part of a tightly connected web.

The conclusion is clear: if we want to improve our memories, we have to make sure we're building robust webs that contain as many associations as possible.

To start using intentional associations in your own learning:

1. **Pick Relevant Associations** – A person, location, object, situation, or emotion can all be associated with what you're trying to learn. Choose whatever method works best for the

item you want to remember. Whatever you choose, it has to be truly *meaningful* to you and your world.

2. **Use Images** – A picture paints a thousand words . . . and reduces your cognitive load! The brain is said to process visual information tens of thousands of times faster than verbal information, so it's important to use pictures, images, and symbols instead of words as associational signals. Details in photos are linked to other areas of the image automatically. If you must use words, try to imagine the words themselves as objects that appeal to your five senses; for example, visualize a mathematical formula where each symbol has a relevant texture, color, and shape that tells you something about its meaning.

3. **Make the Association Concrete and Vivid** – Make associations that are unique, obvious, and relevant to the information you're attempting to remember. In the natural world, your brain learns via all five of your senses. The more vivid the image, the more associations are made and the

stronger the memory. Don't be abstract or vague!

4. **Tie the Association to the Key to be Remembered** – For example, if you have a 2 a.m. flight, make an association between the time and the airplane. How can you do that? You can think of an airplane with a huge number two on it, or you can think of the airplane with two elephants riding on each wing. Or, if you're flying to **Tu**nisia or leaving on a **Tu**esday, you can link the time to the place name.

5. **Make the Association Personal and Add Emotions** – Boring or irrelevant things are easily forgotten, but making a connection personal makes it more meaningful. Emotional associations become strongly established in memory because emotions are processed in the same area of the brain that generates memories (the hippocampus). For example, when associating two with two elephants on the airplane, you can imagine adorable cartoon elephants wearing graduation caps and glasses ("an elephant never forgets"). If you make these cute

elephants a running private joke that you find amusing, you're all the more likely to remember the association.

6. **Repeat a New Association Right Away** – An association, like an original item, must be encoded in order to be recalled. Remember that the more you practice recall, the more firmly embedded the material will be. So, after you've made the association, repeat it a few times immediately and then a few more times later that day. Drilling this way will cement the memory so that when it comes time to recall it for real, your brain already knows what to do. It's like you've firmly linked in the new information to the stable, existing web, so you know it won't budge!

Work with the things your brain is naturally drawn to when creating good memory aids. Things like color and size are fundamental and liable to be remembered most easily, as are things that are absurd, hilarious, or exaggerated. Though you won't see this tip everywhere, making memory cues rude or outright explicit is also a perfect way to cement it in your memory. You're not likely to forget a juicy or shocking bit of information, right? Alternatively, connect them to, uh, private or deeply personal memories that you will have zero problem recalling.

You'll know you've done a good job with making associations when it genuinely feels like recalling new bits of information takes no effort at all.

Don't fall into the trap of trying to construct unnatural and convoluted associations that actually take more time to recall than the original data itself. For example, many students are advised to remember the mnemonic "Please Excuse My Dear Aunt Sally" for the letters of PEMDAS, which help you understand the order of operations in solving mathematical problems (i.e., parenthesis first, then exponents, then multiplication, etc.).

The trouble is, you may be stuck in an exam staring at a math problem and have no idea how to recall the mnemonic itself! Why? Because *Aunt Sally* and the associated sentence are quite arbitrary and mean little. It would be much better to make your own mnemonic that rests on more vivid, meaningful, and concrete associations that come with easy-to-remember images. So, instead, you could remember "Pretty Easy Math Doesn't Actually Suck," which has an emotional component you can really identify with!

Takeaways:

- Retrieval practice is practicing the act of remembering. This is what really matters in learning, since this is the behavior we most want to master and replicate. Try practice tests, feedback, cue cards, summaries, or concept maps.
- Interleaving is a learning technique that involves combining different topics or types of practice to make learning easier. There are many ways to vary practice—for example, varying the kinds of problems, the ways the problems are solved, or the level at which they're solved.
- Chunking is the process of dividing a bigger whole into smaller and more manageable data "chunks." George Miller found that we can only remember approximately seven pieces of information at a time. By grouping, finding patterns, or organizing data, we lower our cognitive load and can process

more. Take each chunk at a time and remember to contextualize it into the bigger picture.

- Deliberately forming associations can boost our memory and deepen our understanding, as well as make learning a lot more fun and engaging. Association is simply the process of connecting new information to information we already know. Strengthen your brain's web of connections by picking personally meaningful associations; imbuing them with vivid sensory imagery; making them personal, concrete, and emotional; and tying that association to the thing you want to remember. Then, practice the association via repetition to drill it.

Chapter 4: How to Deeply Embed New Knowledge

THE FEYNMAN TECHNIQUE

We've covered the optimal attitude to bring to your learning, as well as a few key reading, notetaking, and memorization strategies that will form the basis of your study, whatever you've chosen to learn. **However, learning goes well beyond merely processing and organizing bits of information**. While there's a lot to be said for a good memory and keeping information well managed, some kinds of learning require much, much more from us.

In this chapter, we'll look at several approaches for developing **deep** learning skills within ourselves so that we gain a richer, more sophisticated, and more comprehensive grasp of what we're learning. If we do this, we haven't just learned a topic, but we give ourselves the chance to argue against it, engage with it, or even generate a unique and creative response that's all our own.

The Feynman Technique is a learning method that forces you to develop a richer understanding of a subject, allowing you to reach your full potential. The method was developed by Richard Feynman, an award-winning physicist who won the Nobel Prize in physics. His true superpower, however, was his ability to explain complex subjects to others in simple terms. He realized that jargon, ambiguous language, and complexity reveal a lack of understanding.

The technique is really simple: **First, identify the topic.** Take out a blank sheet of paper once you've decided on a topic. As if you were teaching a child, write down everything you know about the subject you want to understand. **Second, teach it to a child.** Use only simple words and words that a child would comprehend. **Third, identify knowledge gaps.** Examine your notes to ensure you haven't covered any lack of understanding with jargon or glossed over anything difficult. **And fourth, simplify.** Rewrite your explanation in simpler terms.

Sound simple, right? The thing is, the simplicity of this technique is precisely why it's so useful. Even if you are studying very complex topics, you should still be able to summarize what you've understood and convey the main ideas to a person who hasn't studied them. You can only do this if you truly grasp the underlying structure; if you can't explain what you know to others, the idea goes, then you probably don't understand it as well as you think you do!

As you practice this technique, be aware of a very common, very tricky trap: knowing the words and terms to explain a topic doesn't necessarily mean you *understand* it.

It's so tempting to get carried away with jargon and specialist terms and to simply regurgitate second-hand explanations, fooling yourself into believing that this means you really *get* the deeper truths those explanations are pointing to. But how can you say you've learned something and how could you remember it if you don't truly understand it? All you are learning and remembering are superficial concepts and words, not the concept itself.

In using the Feynman technique, the trick is that you are not actually explaining the concept to a child; you're explaining it to *yourself*. Try it and you may be surprised at just how poorly you understand the thing you thought you did.

Let's take a closer look at each step with an example.

First, identify the topic. Feynman invented the entire field of quantum electrodynamics, so don't feel that any topic is too difficult! Let's say you want to explain the concept of natural selection and "survival of the fittest" (a topic many believe they understand but really don't). Pick a simple (not easy, simple) and straightforward topic to focus on. It can be good practice merely to phrase what you're learning in just a few words like this. Pick something you're not just trying to memorize but grasp on a deeper level.

Next, teach this idea to a child. It is not enough to simply give a definition of the topic or an encyclopedia explanation. Feynman said, "The first principle is that you must not fool yourself and you are the easiest person to fool." To uncover gaps in your own understanding, you need to slow down, simplify, and really get a hold of the concept at its most basic.

Imagine a five-year-old child and speak to them using only everyday plain English—no jargon!

"Individuals in a group are all a little bit different. This means some will find it easier to live in their environment than others. If some individuals find it very easy, they may live longer and have more children. We say they are *fit*. Their children will be like them, and that means that the group will, over time, have more and more individuals like that. If an individual finds it too hard to live in that environment, though, it may not have as many children and even die. After a long time, individuals like this are fewer and fewer in the group. The characteristics that make it easy to live, then, become more common. We can say that they have been "selected" for. Individuals who find their environment the easiest to live in will survive, while others won't. This is what *survival of the fittest* means . . ."

As you explain, notice where you are finding yourself tripping up or getting confused.

Maybe you start to notice that you wanted to say something like, "Some individuals adapt to their environment," but as you think about how to simply explain what "adapt" means, you realize that this is actually not true and that you've slightly misunderstood. By using the Feynman technique, you've homed in on a common source of misunderstanding—individuals don't "adapt" in the common, everyday sense of the word. They either die or survive. If you had simply continued to use this term without trying to understand it, you may never have realized the error you were making.

In this way, you look for knowledge gaps and then direct your own learning to fill them. The process is iterative—you could go away and clarify, then return to your hypothetical child to explain again (maybe this time with a diagram!).

If this sounds labor-intensive, then one quick way to use this technique is just to focus on technical terms. Too often we "explain" things to ourselves using other terms that we also don't fully understand. As you read, make sure to highlight key terms, then take the time to explore them properly. The best way to see if you understand a term is to quickly explain it to a non-expert or child *without using any other technical terms*. Once you can do this, continue with your reading. It will save you more time and trouble than you'd first think!

ANALOGIES

Analogies are an important part of human thought and comprehension. Our ability to connect, seek patterns, and find relationships has sparked incredible feats of problem-solving and creativity. Analogies are a tried-and-true method for applying existing knowledge to new concepts, improving our learning.

An analogy highlights one or more parallels between two seemingly unrelated elements. By transferring information from one domain to another, it helps us in establishing new mental models.

Dedre Gentner, professor of psychology and education, explains how "analogical reasoning" is not only something that allows us to learn well, but is in fact what makes human beings so unique among other species. It's what humans do.

An analogy, she claims, is a clever "device for conveying that two situations or domains share relational structure despite arbitrary degrees of difference in the objects that make up the domains." It may be that you found yourself making analogies when using the Feynman technique above. If you can use an analogy such as "a cell is like a water balloon" or "a tesseract is like the three-dimensional shadow of a four-dimensional object, just like the shadow you see on the ground is a two-dimensional shadow of you, a three-dimensional object," you are working in a format your brain naturally uses to learn. Comparing things to other things not only helps you understand them both, but it can also enable you to see new aspects you might not have seen before.

The common format of analogies is "A is like B," with "A" being an unknown abstract notion and "B" being something known, which is typically concrete. To create effective analogies, **first, map the differences between the two domains to check if there are enough connections to make it work.** Next, **evaluate the distinctions between the target and analog concepts, as well as the analogy's**

flaws. Finally, evaluate the new representation.

For example, you could make an analogy such as: the mind is like a sponge.

A is the mind, B is a sponge. Are there enough connections here? Well, both are absorbent, pliant, changeable. Arguably, both can be squeezed out again to release what they contain! So far so good. Good analogies need to be built on something you already know, so the analogy "the gluons holding two up-quarks together in a proton are like the photons exchanged when two particles are electromagnetically charged" will mean nothing if you're not familiar with any of these words!

A good analogy has to emphasize the precise way that two (or more) things are similar— you don't want to get confused and think they are alike in *all* ways. The relationship should be unambiguous and clear so that it aids understanding, not impedes it.

It's best to focus on superficial similarities, not deeper ones, or you may find yourself going down weird rabbit holes that make things more confusing. "The mind is like a sponge" fits these criteria. Obviously, it's *not* like a sponge in many respects, so the analogy is not (and can't be) perfect.

In education, analogies are frequently used to help students, especially younger ones, access new concepts that may be unfamiliar and difficult, by bootstrapping off of ideas they already grasp. In a way, it's Feynman's technique again: if we can understand a basic analogy, we can quickly see the key characteristics of a concept without needing to get stuck in jargon or more explanations that are themselves too high level.

But how can we use analogies when teaching ourselves?

Analogies are both a way to lower cognitive load as well as gain deeper insight into the underlying mechanisms of superficial concepts. Finding an analogy is like finding one "rule" that explains several different instances, which acts to bring the pieces of information down to just one or two. Analogies also boost our memory because it's easier to remember key details when they are in relationship to others and when you know what those details *mean*.

It may feel a little silly at first, but when you first encounter a new and tricky idea, try to break it down into a more manageable shape by finding analogies with other ideas you're already familiar with. For example, you can try to make the mechanisms of cancer a little easier to grasp by imagining that "programs" in certain cells are faulty, causing them to multiply uncontrollably. You can create an extended metaphor of either a faulty computer code or program, or a population boom, both of which are more understandable to you than abstract cell behavior.

Similarly, people can try to understand certain genes as "switches" that turn cancer genes on and off, so they imagine that the "DNA is like a control panel, and this type of cancer is like having a certain switch permanently in the *on* position."

Analogies for self-study are best used:

- in conjunction with the Feynman technique, i.e., can you **simplify** the explanation using a metaphor or simile? This can help you spot gaps in comprehension.
- when you're **reviewing** what you've learned. Constructing an analogy helps you zoom in on the key characteristics.

- when **summarizing** notes to use for memory drilling or retrieval practice later. You could also build analogies into your mind maps or other graphics.

If you find yourself in knots trying to imagine useful analogies, it may be best to try another study technique; the approach should simplify your life, not complicate it. The next time you're engaging with a higher-level topic, simply pause and ask yourself the following questions to help you flesh out useful analogies and metaphors:

What does this process remind you of?

What is its most pronounced features, and can you see that feature repeated in another, unrelated phenomenon?

How can you "translate" this unfamiliar idea into the more familiar symbols of an area you're an expert in?

USE GRAPHIC ORGANIZERS

Another excellent way to lower cognitive load and foster deep learning is to present data in a form your brain loves: pictures. Graphic organizers are visual and graphic presentations that organize thoughts and illustrate connections between diverse facts and concepts. Graphic organizers improve your memory because they simplify and organize. But more than this, they contextualize information and make it *mean* something, giving you access to deeper comprehension.

Many students make the mistake of representing information visually just for the sake of it. But graphics only help your learning when they genuinely add something to your understanding. It's similar to notetaking—the notes themselves don't matter. It's the *way* you take them that counts, and whether that approach is supporting your deeper understanding.

Here are a few common types of graphic organizers you might find handy:

T-Chart

A T-Chart is a diagram that divides ideas into two columns, or looks at two aspects of a single object, concept, or event. Simply divide a page into two columns and title each column. T-charts can be used to compare and contrast, assess the benefits and drawbacks, or weigh up facts versus opinions. They can also be useful for pairing data—for example, listing out the stages of a process on the left and explaining the corresponding purpose of each stage on the right.

Concept Map

A concept map depicts the connections between the main idea and other data. Concepts or ideas are represented by circles or boxes, with arrows connecting them to similar ideas. Some good examples include a diagram showing the hierarchical structure of a business organization (including interactions between each node), a family tree, or a cause-and-effect map that either outlines an actual process (such as oxidative phosphorylation, above) or a potential process (such as a decision map that takes you through choices and outcomes in troubleshooting).

Main Idea Web

The main idea web begins with a central concept and expands to include related concepts and details (or sub-ideas). This form of visual organizer, also known as a spider or semantic map, is generally used for brainstorming and creating ideas for planning or writing purposes. Any time you want to do a "brain dump" and put down everything you know about a topic, you can use this approach.

Main idea webs are a great revision tool, too. At the start of every study session, sit down and try to put down everything you recall from the previous session. Not only does this recall practice strengthen your memory, you also get to see points you may have missed.

Venn Diagram

A Venn diagram is a graphic representation of two or more groups of items that compares and contrasts their similarities and differences in two or more overlapping circles. A circle from one category crosses with a circle from another category to visually show a conceptual overlap between them. So, if your theme of study is the medical diagnosis of several conditions, you may like to quickly represent their relationship with a Venn diagram.

By showing which circles overlap, you show which conditions share symptoms and which symptoms are distinct. For example, all five conditions share "inflammation markers" as a symptom, and so all five circles intersect here, where you write "inflammation" in the center. For those symptoms that appear only within one condition, you place it alone in the circle not intersecting with the others. In this way, you see complex relationships at a glance.

Sequence Chart

A sequence chart (also known as a flow diagram) depicts a succession of actions or events in chronological order. This can help you understand a story's sequence of events and make clear the cause and effect (or problem and solution) linkages among several events in a text. So, as you read an essay about a series of historical events, you may jot down your own simplified sequence chart to trace the events in chronological order.

If you decide to use arrows, you can imply cause and effect. Several arrows from different boxes arriving at the same result quickly show that an outcome had a multifactorial origin, for example. This is not unlike chunking, since you are taking what may be several paragraphs long and condensing it down to the cause-and-effect essence.

Mind Mapping

Perhaps the most well-known of visual organizing strategies is mind mapping. By providing an overview and summary of a body of knowledge and combining words and images, this technique helps us structure, organize, memorize, arrange, revise, brainstorm, and learn information.

Mind mapping combines logic and creativity to help us think more clearly and effectively about the subject we're studying. The process of creating a mind map is fairly straightforward. All that's required is an *understanding of the structure* beneath that topic. In fact, you may find that clarifying this structure in order to make a mind map is a useful exercise in itself and will help you better grasp what you're learning.

Be warned, though: mind maps are intuitive and take little explanation, but not all mind maps are equal, and it is possible to create one that adds little to your learning. Many students waste time making mind maps that *look* nice but don't add any insight into the underlying structure of the information they represent.

Here are some tips to creating a mind map that really does its job:

1. Take out a sheet of paper and place it horizontally in front of you.
2. Draw a reasonably sized, memorable central image or symbol that represents the topic you are going to be mapping. Alternatively, draw a circle and write some words inside the circle to represent that topic.
3. Draw at least four thick branches radiating outward from the central image. Using a different color for each branch is helpful. These branches represent the secondary aspects of the topic.
4. Write keywords (headings) along these branches that represent the central image and the topic you are mapping.
5. Draw additional branches that extend from your main branches. The words on these branches are sub-topics of the words you wrote on your main branches.
6. Keep expanding the mind map outward with additional sub sub-topics/keywords and branches.

Sounds simple, but you really need to pay attention to the *relationships* between each of these branches and sub-branches. Just like a literal map needs to have a good resemblance to the territory it represents, your mind map needs to accurately reflect the organization of the topic at hand—and its relative proportions! That means similar concepts must be grouped together, and dissimilar ones put as far away from each other as possible. You want core topics to be at the center of the mind map, with less important details the further out you go.

If you find that one branch is getting too heavy while others are sparse, it may be time to ask whether you need to update your understanding. Draw another map, perhaps this time breaking the heavy branch down into smaller sub-branches. Try to keep your level of detail consistent; for example, don't go into excruciating detail on one branch, noting every little fact, but then on another branch list only broad categories that you don't explore further.

To get the most out of mind maps, use the visual space to its fullest by adding color, pictures, arrows, or symbols. Vary the size, style, and shape of your lettering to convey information. Draw links between branches to show their relationship, or even include other visual organizing techniques inside the mind map.

For example, you could modify one branch so that it is actually a decision tree or process map. Use different-shaped nodes as a shorthand (for example, a square for a fact, a circle for a process) and include mnemonics, little jokes, scribbles, and other doodles that quickly capture more complex concepts. On a mind map about oxidative phosphorylation, you could have the repeated symbol of a cartoon ox, maybe with each of his limbs representing a key feature of the process. Whatever you decide on, mind mapping will work if you make consistent associations, and you make them graphically.

CONNECT, EXTEND, CHALLENGE

Connect, Extend, Challenge is one excellent way to make useful associations and can help you relate new ideas and facts to what you already know about a topic, deepening learning. By doing this method, you'll become more deliberate and autonomous as a learner, but beyond this, you will also gain a deeper and richer comprehension of your chosen topic. Whereas making simple associations is a great way to remember the time your plane leaves or recall the order of the PEDMAS mnemonic, you may need to go a little further when more complex concepts are involved.

Connect, Extend, Challenge is a technique that will develop your metacognition skills, or your ability to think about your thinking, and learn about your learning. This strategy is most effective when you've been introduced to new perspectives that may question your prior understanding or shed new light on it.

Here's how it's done:

Step 1: Connect

Whether you've read something new or encountered a novel technique, idea, or opinion, just take a moment to get familiar with the material before attempting to connect it to what you already know. Then ask yourself, *how does this new thing relate to what you already know?*

There may be another familiar thinker whose theories sound similar, there may be a previous event or problem that reminds you of this one, or you may simply find yourself thinking of one or two concepts that seem the same, at least superficially. For example, in a history lesson when learning about a completely new area of study (let's say the Mexican-American war), you may start to see similarities in the narratives of the history you've already learned (the American Civil War).

Step 2: Extend

Next ask, *how does this current piece of information extend your current thinking?*

For example, you may not have been aware that Texas declared independence from the Republic of Mexico in 1836, and the effect this had on both countries in the subsequent years. You might have always assumed that the prime cause for the American Civil War was the legitimacy of slavery, but as you read more about the Mexican-American war, you realize that it wasn't just the existence of slavery in certain areas, but its *expansion* into other areas, such as Texas.

By incorporating the new information into the old, you are creating a bigger, metanarrative that holds it all. Essentially, you are updating your old model rather than merely tacking on new pieces of data. In the process, your memory is improved, but more importantly, your overall understanding is deepened.

Step 3: Challenge

Ask yourself, *does this new information challenge your existing comprehension?* Take a look to see if any new questions emerge for you, or if any misconceptions are coming to light. Many math and science students naturally discover this as they advance in their learning, i.e., that the things they were taught in school aren't all that true anymore!

Of course, you may have guessed that this technique isn't appropriate for every subject or topic. Sometimes, a simple mnemonic or image will do the trick to spur your memory, but sometimes you'll need to grapple with material at a deeper level.

Connect, Extend, Challenge is perfect for qualitative subjects like history, English literature, politics, psychology, sociology, art, or philosophy. But it can definitely be used for more technical subjects like music, math, and science, provided the topic is at a high enough abstract level.

Teachers will often use this format when they want to encourage students to develop their critical thinking skills, but for self-directed learners, it's also an ideal way to gain a deeper appreciation of what you're learning. Remember the webs that make up your long-term memory? Every time you learn something new, it's as though you're inserting in new nodes and connections, unraveling some sections of the web, and re-stitching others. If you simply dump new information on top of the old without modifying what you already know, you miss a chance to make meaningful associations. If your learning is shallow, then your memory will be weaker.

Finally, one very obvious and concrete way to use this technique is to literally make room in your notes for new information, or extend a mnemonic or memory device to include another piece. You can imagine that what you already know is a pre-existing scaffold, and the new things you learn can be attached to that scaffold as you go. For example, leave room on your written notes so you can return to them later. When you annotate them, use a different-colored pen or a specific color to indicate that you have since updated or extended your understanding. That way, your final notes are not just summaries of information, they're archives of the learning process itself.

So long as you compare what you are learning with what you've already learned, you are anchoring yourself in something concrete and your memory will improve, along with your depth understanding. We'll explore this topic to its fullest in our next and final chapter.

Takeaways:

- Some subjects will require more than mere data processing, but need a richer, more sophisticated, and more comprehensive understanding, i.e., deep learning. The Feynman Technique is a learning method that forces you to develop a richer understanding of a subject. To identify any gaps in your own understanding, explain your topic to a child without using any additional jargon.
- Analogies are an important part of human thought and comprehension.

Seeking patterns and finding relationships help us apply existing knowledge to new concepts, improving our learning. Use the format "A is like B." Use analogies when you want to simplify (such as in the Feynman technique), review, or summarize. Not every topic lends itself to analogies!
- Another excellent way to lower cognitive load and foster deep learning is to present data in a form your brain loves: pictures. Graphic organizers improvise memory but also deeper understanding. Examples include T-charts, concept maps, main idea webs, Venn diagrams, sequence charts, and mind mapping. You could combine many of these or create your own hybrid. What is important is that you are conveying underlying organization of the concepts graphically and visually.
- Connect, Extend, Challenge is an excellent way to make useful associations and can help you relate new ideas and facts to what you already know about a topic, deepening learning. This is a metacognitive skill that will cement your new learning into the web of your current understanding. Ask, 1) how does

this new thing relate to what you already know? 2) how does this current piece of information extend your current thinking? and 3) does this new information challenge your existing comprehension?

Chapter 5: The Bigger Picture of Using Your Knowledge

KWL

At this point, having discussed so many different techniques, approaches, and strategies, you may be wondering just how to bring everything together. Should you use *all* the techniques? The answer is no!

In this chapter, we're looking at how to take everything we've learned and bring it together to form a strategy that is simple and manageable but also effective. One simple way to keep organized is to use the KWL approach.

KWL (Know, Want-to-Know, and Learned) is a useful acronym not just for reading with purpose, but for helping you stay organized as you plan your study

program. This approach is primarily used to organize your study process and stay tuned into your sense of purpose, but it's also a surprisingly effective way to boost memory. This is because you're constantly inviting yourself to check in with what has made it into long-term memory banks, what hasn't, and what you'd like to do about it. This technique only takes a few minutes but will spare you from drilling material you already know and missing material that needed more of your attention.

Simply draw three columns on a page and title them, "What I know," "What I want to know," and "What I learned."

Now you can use this chart both before and after your learning to help you keep track of your progress and stay focused on your goals. Like the main idea web, this technique helps you discern between what has already been understood and what is still being mastered. This alone lets you shape your path forward.

In **Know**, make a list of everything you know about the current topic. What have you already learned, heard, or experienced about the subject? What is the situation?

What is the author's name? When was the text written? Who published it and why?

Imagine you are getting a "lay of the land" and sketching out the boundaries of a new realm you're exploring. This step could consolidate the learning you've already done on this topic, or it can be a nice starting point for a completely new topic (in fact, you may be surprised by just how much you already know about even brand-new topics!).

In **Want-To-Know**, continue your pre-reading preparations by making a list of what you want to learn after your learning session. Don't just jump in! What exactly do you want to know? Use the questions who, where, what, why, when, and how. This is like charting a route through the new territory.

What you write in this column could be about your personal objectives, but, in academic reading, it's more likely to be about what you need to learn from the reading for your class. Either way, you need the focus that a few goals will bring.

Even before you dive in to read or investigate, can you find ways to connect what you want to know with what you already know? Are you expecting to have your preconceived ideas challenged in any way?

In **Learned**, you answer and record the questions you posed above. As you read or study, make a list of the text's essential points as well as anything surprising, contentious, or difficult to understand. Compare and contrast what you are learning both with what you wanted to know and what you already know. Have you achieved what you set out to achieve? Have you found ways to correct previous misunderstandings or expand a previously limited view?

The KWL approach is really all about reminding yourself of your ultimate learning goal: to continually master the things you currently don't understand. Here's a few examples to show how flexible this approach is and how it can be used in different ways:

Example 1

Before reading a new and difficult journal article, you take a separate piece of paper and draw 3 KWL columns. You intend to use the SQ3R technique to focus on the most important info, the Feynman technique to make sure you're understanding things on a deeper level, and semantic feature analysis to compare and contrast some of the points in the text. You then plan to incorporate this feature analysis into a broader mind map.

However, you keep all of these strategies organized by using KWL. You start by reviewing what you know (maybe very little!), and then you make a list of all the questions you have, i.e., what you want to know. This can be combined with the survey and question part of SQ3R. Then, you read the text, and as you go, you keep coming back to what you want to know.

As you find out the answers, you tick them off the list. You decide you will stop reading when you have transferred everything in the "want to know" column to the "learned" column.

Example 2

Let's say it's the end of a six-month period of study and you've been working hard on a certain topic. But now it's time to wrap up, revise, and set goals for the next module. You set up a KWL table and ask yourself, generally, what you know about the entire topic. You list all the things you're super confident about.

In the next column, you list the concepts that you're still unclear about. You take this list and use it to help you devise a revision plan (why not let it help you design a retrieval practice, or practice only those practice problems you have the most trouble with?). You decide that you've revised enough when you've cleared the "want to know" column.

Example 3

Perhaps you incorporate gamification into your KWL table. Every week, you take a look at a KWL chart hung on your wall where you make a big ritual of crossing off items from the "want to know" column.

Every new piece you can honestly add to the "learned" column can earn a star, which you later redeem for "prizes." For example, for every three concepts moved into the "learned" column, you give yourself a well-earned break where you enjoy a hobby or have a healthy treat. In this way, the KWL approach is not just keeping you organized and focused, it's also keeping you motivated!

TRIANGLE-SQUARE-CIRCLE

Too often, students of all kinds will get bogged down in the details of their study journey and lose sight of their broader goals. Because they never "come up for air," they don't have enough time to pause, consolidate what is learned, and absorb any new lessons. If you rush along from one technique to another or from one lesson to the next, you may not be allowing your brain enough time to properly process what it's learning. To keep the journey metaphor going, it's as though you are walking a long route, eyes on the road, never gazing upward to see if you're still on the right track or how far you've come!

Triangle-Square-Circle is a technique not unlike KWL in that it forces you to take short breaks during the learning process and assess what you know, what you don't, and what steps you're going to take next. The approach rests on road sign symbols:

1. Draw a **triangle** and extract "three important points" from what you've read or studied.

2. Then, draw a **square** and note any assertions, concepts, ideas, or perspectives about the lesson that "square" with you, i.e., are in agreement with your general view or else confirm what you already know.

3. Lastly, draw a **circle** and write down any questions or responses that have been "circling" in your head.

Like KWL, this quick technique will help you gain a sense of where you are, reinforce what's been learned, and get an idea of what still needs your attention. Like KWL, though, its strength is actually broader than this: it gets you into a proactive self-directed mindset where your study can be optimized.

Too many students get lost following rabbit holes. Either they waste time studying things they already understand thoroughly (simply because they like feeling like they understand) or they focus too heavily on everything they still need to master, becoming overwhelmed and forgetting just how far they have come. Finally, some students lose focus because they are not being honest about the effectiveness of their approach—i.e., what they're doing is simply not working, but they never stop long enough to notice it.

If you deliberately build in time for reflection and metacognition (i.e., with this technique or KWL), you are giving yourself the opportunity to make minor course corrections before they become bigger problems in comprehension. When you are a self-directed learner, you keep track of your progress, you take charge of your own learning, and you *continuously* reflect on the results you're getting. If you are studying alone and without any external feedback, it's especially important to give yourself time to process, articulate, and reflect on your journey—and make changes as necessary.

At first, the triangle-square-circle approach may seem too basic—could it really add anything to your learning? But just try it and you'll see how much can be gained by slowing down and deliberately spelling out what is going on at every stage of your process. It might look like this:

You are learning about the history of women's rights in the United States from a legal point of view and are working your way through a series of books on the subject, all written by very different authors with very different perspectives. You encounter a new book that expressly argues against the philosophical position of Rousseau and examines the rise of his way of thinking as reflected through various important legal cases throughout history. After you read a chapter, you stop and contemplate.

You take a piece of paper and quickly draw your triangle, seeing if you can extract three main ideas from what you've just encountered. Granted, you may have encountered *many* ideas, but you choose the three that are most pertinent to you right now. You write down three concepts: 1) Rousseau's overall conception of human nature, 2) the differences in the fundamental natures of men and women, and 3) what Rousseau believed this implied for women's education.

Then, you draw your square. You identify four things that you agree with, understand, and can adopt into your own worldview. You note that there are several points you agree with both Rousseau and the points the author is making, or at least, they don't seem too alien to you.

However, in reading, you can't help but notice that there are some emerging questions and objections. You draw a circle and write down a note inside it: Rousseau thought that women didn't require education because their main purpose in life was to stay at home and raise children. But if they are fundamentally irrational and uneducated, how could they educate their children? Perhaps you also start mulling over the idea that, if Rousseau as an Enlightenment thinker championed democracy, equality, and liberty, how could he also argue for the subjugation of half the population?

As you can see, the triangle-square-circle process offers the same opportunity to check in with our progress, but lets us take things deeper. It invites us to **engage**—not only with the material but also with our own understanding of it.

In the above example, the three shapes allow you to broadly summarize what you've read, connect it to what you already know, and start to generate questions that allow you to probe more deeply into what you're dealing with. Had you *not* done this process, you may have never given your mind time to formulate its own unique response to the material. You would have had a shallower (therefore harder to remember) grasp on the topic.

Of course, this technique can also be used for keeping track of simpler things, too. For example:

Triangle – you quickly ask the three main points being made in a fun TED talk you've just watched.

Square – you take note of two other talks/speakers/authors that it reminds you of, and two related theories that you already know about.

Circle – you find yourself with a question that the TED talk hasn't answered for you.

What you do after a triangle-square-circle analysis depends on what emerged for you. In the above example, you may decide that your next move is to find an answer to your question. Or, in the previous example, you may find that you'd like to find more material from critics of Rousseau, to see if your objections are more fully explored elsewhere by other thinkers.

Successful and effective self-directed learners engage in this kind of process naturally. They never just drill information or swallow it uncritically. They are constantly picking it apart, turning it over in their minds, contextualizing it, asking it questions, and allowing their curiosity to drive their next steps. Both the triangle-square-circle technique and KWL teach you to take this proactive approach to your own learning.

BUILD A SECOND BRAIN

Many thousands of years ago, mankind figured out something that would change the trajectory of their evolution forever: they made marks on a page or clay tablet and eventually devised written language. What used to be stored in human memory and oral tradition was suddenly able to be kept outside the brain in written form. It's hard to appreciate today what a quantum leap this was for our ancestors; it drastically increased *how much* we could grab hold of, store, process, and analyze.

This is the big idea behind the concept of building a "second brain." As we've seen, the human brain has natural cognitive limitations. But in effect, every technique we've considered is a tool that helps us *augment* this brain and get around its limitations.

If you're the kind of person who is drawn to personal development, improving your skills, and progressing in your learning (whatever that looks like for you), then you've definitely come up against the limits of your own brain. You may have encountered amazing pieces of information and simply forgotten them, or had great insights and shifts in understanding that you nevertheless didn't document or take action on. We are now swimming in a world filled with more information than our ancestors could have dreamed of—and yet most of us still fail to make effective use of any of it!

A second brain is a way to save the insights, information, learning, and progress we gather. In the same way as writing something down allowed our ancestors to remember much, much more than they could before, a second brain is a deliberate and systematic way to process and order all the information we come across in life. A second brain is two important things:

- External
- Centralized

You may have plenty of information in your world, but it might be spread across different technologies and formats—articles, books, audiobooks, videos, images, memos, webinars . . . In other words, it's external but not centralized. On the other hand, you may have tons of information in one place (your head), but so long as it's in there, it's subject to the narrow limitations of your memory, i.e., it's centralized but not external.

With a second brain, you keep all relevant content in one, external place so it doesn't overwhelm you and become impractical. You consolidate everything in one grand meta-plan. Not only do you keep organized, but you see how you can direct all this information to one single, practical aim—your learning goals.

You have a record of everything you've encountered and can use it to direct **actions** in your world. Instead of being scattered and ineffective, we put everything to work and start achieving our bigger, more pressing life goals, such as upskilling professionally, personal development, or simply gaining mastery in a chosen area.

With the second brain doing the grunt work, our biological brain is free to do what it does best: encounter and process fresh information. We lessen the cognitive load of having to remember things by passing them over to technology to remember for us. However, it's not enough just to lazily assume "technology" will solve all your problems and do all your work for you. A good second brain system must:

- Continually move projects to their completion, i.e., it must be *results oriented*.
- Have a means to identify patterns, connections, relationships, and overlaps, i.e., information must be stored *meaningfully*.
- Relieve stress and make things *easier and simpler*—be careful, many tech solutions are actually more complex than the problem they're trying to solve!
- Develop your skill and expertise, i.e., help you to refine what you already know how to do. The idea is not to become passive and lazy, but to become *more focused and masterful.*
- Favor quality over quantity. Be discerning and collect a wealth of knowledge that has real-world *value* for you.
- Be flexible. Learning is life long, and your second brain needs to be up to the task of constantly *evolving* with you.

So, all that said, what does creating a second brain actually look like?

In our book so far, we've considered smaller, more localized tips and tricks for improving the learning process. Now we end our book with a *meta-technique*, i.e., one that brings all these techniques together.

Remembering that it needs to be external and centralized, we have a lot of power over how we design our second brain. In essence, though, we need a single place where we can store our emerging insights, note and notice patterns and connections, see how new information connects to old information, and periodically assess the current store of knowledge—is it still contributing to life's bigger goals?

Step 1: Collect and organize

The internet flings information at us at a dizzying rate, but much of it disappears immediately; we scroll by and instantly forget. Instead, think like a collector or curator and consciously capture the information that has most value for you. When you encounter something fascinating online, don't just dive in. Save it and store it away where you can keep it and access it later.

You could try organizing apps like Evernote or construct your own system of Google

Docs. Assign a different folder or file to each topic, project, or goal. Be careful here and make sure you're not bogging yourself down with irrelevant material—choose only what resonates and what is directly applicable to your goals at hand. You could have a miscellaneous folder with things that *might* be interesting at some point, but don't let them distract from the most important pieces of information.

Decide on a threshold for what makes it into your repository.

Does this add to your life in any way?

Do you find this inherently intriguing?

Does this connect to and enrich what you're currently dealing with?

Are you instinctively drawn to it, or does it challenge you in some way?

As you learn, you'll be making notes of your own, too. Collect these and integrate them. Make summaries, mind maps, or visual organizers specifically to include in your collection.

Remember your learning journal? This can form the more emotional, self-reflective part of your process. Think of yourself as compiling your own curriculum for a broader study program you design for yourself—a study program where the outcome is to be the best version of yourself.

Step 2: Make connections

Your brain is built on associations, and your second brain should be, too.

As you collect and compile, you will automatically start to notice patterns emerging. See what insights are suggesting themselves. An article may remind you of a video someone recommended. A colleague might mention an idea that you encountered a few weeks back, and you may decide to follow it up, but by incorporating yet a third concept you've just recently started exploring.

Without a second brain, these ideas are fun but fleeting "what ifs" that don't go anywhere. With a second brain, they become powerful ways to optimize, be creative, and explore new opportunities.

Write notes and materials with your future self in mind. As you collect, highlight key terms and their definitions so you can see at a glance what they mean next time you read through the notes. Make mini summaries wherever you can. Add useful links, helpful diagrams, or contact information you might forget later. These are like breadcrumbs for you to quickly find your way back to important information later.

One thing to practice is "progressive summarization." Your organic brain works by condensing and chunking, so do the same with your second brain. A progressive summary is concentrating the main points of a piece in stages, over time.

For example, you make summaries of a few books, but later collect only the best summaries and further distil their main features into one or two sentences to give you a mega-summary of all the books. However, keep the previous summaries. This way, you can examine your material at any level of detail, depending on your needs.

You can zoom in and find the original, full-length piece, or you can look at the summary, or you can zoom right out and examine the bigger picture this article is a part of. Achieving something like this without writing anything down is extremely difficult!

If all of this sounds stressful, it shouldn't. Your notes will ideally be formed gradually one bit at a time. If you stress yourself out trying to compile a giant meta-structure all at once, you'll get overwhelmed and probably do a bad job anyway. Instead, be *opportunistic* and add to your notes when it's natural and easy to do so. Be patient and build things up organically. The notes are there to serve you—not the other way around.

A good rule of thumb is to continue to think in terms of value. If a note doesn't add value, ditch it. More importantly, *every time you touch a note, make sure you are doing so in a way that adds value.* In other words, if you are just endlessly organizing and reorganizing the same notes without any benefit, you're wasting time.

Spread out the workload and make sure that the most important and most frequently used notes are most accessible.

Step 3: Create

You are not reading, learning, capturing, summarizing, synthesizing, and analyzing just for the sake of it. There is a broader *purpose* behind what you're doing. Do all your efforts speak to that purpose?

Your goals may be set for you by others (passing exams, for example) or set yourself.

They may be small (learn to do one specific thing) or broader (become a better critical thinker). Whatever they are, they need to inspire and direct your learning, and likewise all your learning needs to be focused on that goal. This is where KWL and triangle-square-circle come in handy, as they allow us to appraise our process and measure it against our overarching goals.

There's another great advantage to a second brain, though, and that is that it allows you to be genuinely creative. When you've been gathering and synthesizing for a while, you can't help but notice patterns, and these patterns then start to suggest interesting new avenues, a bold solution, or a fun new possibility to explore. Draw on the big themes and then add your own perspective, expanding on the ideas.

Second Brain Rules to Follow

Your second brain will work best when it suits you, your lifestyle, your chosen area of study, and your goals. But it should still follow a few key rules to be effective:

1. Put knowledge to use—don't be passive and stay in research mode forever. Process what you encounter and turn it into concrete **action** that

addresses your real-world goals. Constantly ask what you can create or what changes as a result of what you've learned.
2. Don't get overwhelmed. The key is to chunk information, summarize, condense, and work with smaller units, not bigger ones. Go slow and be patient.
3. Avoid perfectionism. Your goal is not to make a one hundred percent complete and pretty-looking archive of static information, but to create a living, breathing repository that responds dynamically to real life. That's going to be a bit messy at times!
4. Don't work in isolation. Connect with others, share your insights, ask questions, get a mentor, or actively teach and coach others. Knowledge and expertise strengthen when they're put out into the real world. Don't be afraid to collaborate or get feedback.

If you cultivate the discipline needed to start building a second brain today, you will be astonished when you look back at it a year or two later. You will see interesting conversations come to life in new projects and connections. You will see questions inspiring reading and learning, which in turn fuel more questions that lead you to brilliant insights, solutions, and endeavors you would never have considered before.

You will see that information hasn't just flitted across your path and disappeared; instead, you have captured it, processed it, and made the very best of it. A second brain is not only about storage or organization or learning. On a deeper level, it's about having a tool that encourages genuine and sophisticated engagement with the world.

We started our book talking about the characteristics of a self-directed learner. Practice the techniques in this book as well as the overarching second brain strategy, and you will find that your own brain starts to change. The way you look at information will shift, and you will discover a whole new world of active, responsible engagement that is a thousand times richer than you could have imagined. You become a better student but also a better self-teacher. You become disciplined, autonomous, and resourceful. You begin to *love* learning.

In school, we were all taught a style of learning that many would argue we now need to consciously un-teach ourselves! In practicing the techniques described in these pages, the hope is that you cultivate something more valuable than a specific skill or store of knowledge. Instead, you develop your own capacity for learning in itself.

Once you are a skilled and masterful learner, there is no limit to what you can apply yourself to.

Takeaways:

- You need a broad, meta-strategy in which to embed all the different tips and tricks covered. KWL (Know, Want-to-Know, and Learned) is a useful acronym not just for reading with purpose, but for helping you stay organized as you plan your broader study program. Draw three columns and, as you learn, constantly compare what you want to know with what you are actually learning.
- Triangle-Square-Circle is a similar technique that forces you to take short breaks during learning and assess what you know, what you don't, and what steps you're going to take next. Draw a

triangle and extract "three important points," draw a square and note any ideas that "square" with you, and draw a circle for questions or responses that are still "circling" in your head.
- In both KWL and Triangle-Square-Circle, what matters is that we actively and consciously engage with the material we learn and become self-directed learners.
- The human brain has natural cognitive limitations, but we can *augment* this brain and get around its limitations by creating a second brain. A second brain is a way to save the insights, information, learning, and progress externally and in a centralized manner, making us not just better learners but more effective people in general.
- Collect and organize, make connections, and then create. It will take time to build a second brain, so be patient, be opportunistic, and break things into manageable chunks. Constantly condense material, look for patterns, and ask how you can apply what you've learned. Finally, don't work in isolation—

collaboration, feedback, and mentorship can be invaluable.

Summary Guide

CHAPTER 1: THE RIGHT ATTITUDE

- The evidence-based scientific facts tell us that our conventional understanding about learning is sometimes wrong. It's a good idea to be clear about the study approaches you've used so far and be honest about how well those are actually serving you. It may be time to try something completely new!
- Self-directed learning is as much about useful methods as it is about attitude, mood, perception, and feeling. It is important to cultivate the right mindset when it comes to learning. A self-directed learner is ideally playful, autonomous, open to experience, flexible, self-

accepting, and capable of internal evaluation and motivation. Identify your goals, stay curious, challenge yourself, track your progress, be intrinsically motivated, collaborate with others, and keep a "study journal" to actively reflect on your progress.
- According to Gibbs, it is only when we actively reflect on our experiences that we truly learn. We can use his "structured debriefing process": **describe** the factual situation, describe our **feelings** about it, **evaluate** the experience, make an **analysis**, arrive at two **conclusions** (one general, one specific), and formulate an **action plan** for next time.
- The brain has natural and inbuilt limits to the amount of new information it can take in, and we cannot overload it. Long-term memory is the bottle, and short-term memory is the narrow spout. We can lower cognitive load by condensing, limiting distractions, and having enough breaks.
- Gamification means incorporating gaming mechanics into learning to boost motivation and engagement. Remember,

though, that internal motivation is ultimately more powerful, so try to include elements of **mastery, autonomy, and purpose** in your learning.

CHAPTER 2: DEVELOPING READING, NOTE-TAKING, AND WRITING SKILLS

- Reading, writing, and notetaking are likely to be key skills in your learning journey. The SQ3R technique helps you identify the most important parts of anything you read: follow the steps of survey, question, read, recite, and review to help you break more complex texts down into manageable chunks. Repeat the process as a continuous cycle.
- One simple summarizing tool that can help you engage with material is the 3-2-1 strategy. It involves summarizing key ideas, rethinking them, and posing a question to reveal uncertainty. List three things you found out, two interesting things that made you curious, and one question you still have. This helps you

process rather than just passively absorb information.
- A tool that can help us analyze difficult new academic terms and understand their underlying concepts is something called the Frayer Model. Create a simple four-square chart that outlines a word's **definition**, characteristics, **examples,** and **non-examples** to help you fine-tune your understanding.
- Semantic Feature Analysis is another method that helps you get a good grip on new terms and uses a grid to explore the *relationships* between terms and the features those terms possess. Create a grid with concepts along the side and features along the top to compare and contrast their characteristics. This may allow you to make predictions or find patterns.
- Better notes will help you remember concepts, develop useful learning skills, and better comprehend a subject. There are several useful notetaking strategies to experiment with: the Cornell method, the mapping method, the outlining method, the charting method, and the sentence method—or a combination of these.

- Use "writing to learn" by writing essays according to RAFT prompts, which help you understand the purpose and function of a text. **R**ole: Who is the writer and what is their role? **A**udience: To whom are you writing? **F**ormat: Are you writing to persuade, entertain, inform, or describe? Something else? **T**opic: What are you writing about?

CHAPTER 3: BOOSTING MEMORY

- Retrieval practice is practicing the act of remembering. This is what really matters in learning, since this is the behavior we most want to master and replicate. Try practice tests, feedback, cue cards, summaries, or concept maps.
- Interleaving is a learning technique that involves combining different topics or types of practice to make learning easier. There are many ways to vary practice—for example, varying the kinds of problems, the ways the problems are solved, or the level at which they're solved.

- Chunking is the process of dividing a bigger whole into smaller and more manageable data "chunks." George Miller found that we can only remember approximately seven pieces of information at a time. By grouping, finding patterns, or organizing data, we lower our cognitive load and can process more. Take each chunk at a time and remember to contextualize it into the bigger picture.
- Deliberately forming associations can boost our memory and deepen our understanding, as well as make learning a lot more fun and engaging. Association is simply the process of connecting new information to information we already know. Strengthen your brain's web of connections by picking personally meaningful associations; imbuing them with vivid sensory imagery; making them personal, concrete, and emotional; and tying that association to the thing you want to remember. Then, practice the association via repetition to drill it.

CHAPTER 4: DEEP LEARNING APPROACHES

- Some subjects will require more than mere data processing, but need a richer, more sophisticated, and more comprehensive understanding, i.e., deep learning. The Feynman Technique is a learning method that forces you to develop a richer understanding of a subject. To identify any gaps in your own understanding, explain your topic to a child without using any additional jargon.
- Analogies are an important part of human thought and comprehension. Seeking patterns and finding relationships help us apply existing knowledge to new concepts, improving our learning. Use the format "A is like B." Use analogies when you want to simplify (such as in the Feynman technique), review, or summarize. Not every topic lends itself to analogies!
- Another excellent way to lower cognitive load and foster deep learning is to present data in a form your brain loves: pictures. Graphic organizers improvise memory but also deeper understanding. Examples include T-charts, concept maps, main idea webs, Venn diagrams,

sequence charts, and mind mapping. You could combine many of these or create your own hybrid. What is important is that you are conveying underlying organization of the concepts graphically and visually.
- Connect, Extend, Challenge is an excellent way to make useful associations and can help you relate new ideas and facts to what you already know about a topic, deepening learning. This is a metacognitive skill that will cement your new learning into the web of your current understanding. Ask, 1) how does this new thing relate to what you already know? 2) how does this current piece of information extend your current thinking? and 3) does this new information challenge your existing comprehension?

CHAPTER 5: THE BIGGER PICTURE

- You need a broad, meta-strategy in which to embed all the different tips and tricks covered. KWL (Know, Want-to-Know, and Learned) is a useful acronym not just

for reading with purpose, but for helping you stay organized as you plan your broader study program. Draw three columns and, as you learn, constantly compare what you want to know with what you are actually learning.
- Triangle-Square-Circle is a similar technique that forces you to take short breaks during learning and assess what you know, what you don't, and what steps you're going to take next. Draw a triangle and extract "three important points," draw a square and note any ideas that "square" with you, and draw a circle for questions or responses that are still "circling" in your head.
- In both KWL and Triangle-Square-Circle, what matters is that we actively and consciously engage with the material we learn and become self-directed learners.
- The human brain has natural cognitive limitations, but we can *augment* this brain and get around its limitations by creating a second brain. A second brain is a way to save the insights, information, learning, and progress externally and in a centralized manner, making us not just

better learners but more effective people in general.
- Collect and organize, make connections, and then create. It will take time to build a second brain, so be patient, be opportunistic, and break things into manageable chunks. Constantly condense material, look for patterns, and ask how you can apply what you've learned. Finally, don't work in isolation—collaboration, feedback, and mentorship can be invaluable.

www.ingramcontent.com/pod-product-compliance
Lightning Source LLC
Chambersburg PA
CBHW020531080526
44583CB00013B/814